Kevin's Story:
Love Will Make Them Stronger

Carol A. Farrell

Jackie,
you were such a cheerleader
and spirit-lifter during
Kevin's long illness!
Thank you for a
lifetime of friendship,
love and support.
With my love,
Carol

For Connor and KerryAnne

TRAMPOLINE

If anything he looked like an exuberant frog mid-way through a leap, legs drawn up akimbo, arms extended outward and upward, propelled sky-ward from a hard bounce on the trampoline. Who would have recognized him for the 30 year old engineer he was! Kevin sent two of his young nephews even higher, all of them shrieking with laughter.

It was Easter Sunday 2003, and the family had gathered that afternoon for the annual egg hunt, feasting and fun. The food was all predictable: the cheese/Dorito dip and veggies that preceded ham, scalloped potatoes, fruit salad, deviled eggs. It was all topped off with the traditional bunny cake which Kathy always provided for our main dessert.

Our egg hunt had two parts: the children stayed inside, away from all windows while the adults hid the eggs in flower beds, palm fronds and the tail pipes of cars parked in the driveway. The big prize was finding the egg with the dollar bill inside. Of course there was a special prize for the one who found the most eggs.

Later in that afternoon Kevin and Kathleen had distributed a plastic egg to each family and asked us all to open them at the same time. Inside we found a photo of almost one year old Connor wearing a t-shirt announcing that he was soon to become a Big Brother! Cheers and hugs all around!

It was the last joyful family gathering we were to have before our world crashed a mere month later.

Email of October 4, 2004

Dear Friends,

Sixteen months ago, when it first became evident that Kevin was dealing with a very serious illness, I did what every mother would do: I prayed. Almost in the same breath of that first prayer, I began to contact our friends to pray with us that this thing we dreaded would not be. Over the months I asked for prayers for many things, above all, for the miracle of a return to health and a long life for Kevin. Over the months, you joined us and together we petitioned God, expecting that this miracle would surely come.

But it was not to be.

Sleepless nights and days filled with both hope and despair gave me ample opportunity to examine my beliefs about life and death, prayer and God. I have distilled them down to these two: God is good and wants only good for us, and that life is imperfect and needs our help.

We are not angry at God that our prayers for Kevin were not answered in the way we hoped. We wish with all our hearts that it were otherwise but we do not fault God. I believe that his desire for Kevin, and for each of us, is wholeness in body, mind and spirit.

I am no longer as sure as I once was about how prayer works or what it is fair to expect prayer to do. What I do know, beyond a shadow of a doubt, is that all of us, especially Kevin and Kathleen, were blessed with the courage and strength needed to meet the challenges of this terrible time. I know that all of us who prayed were drawn closer to each other, and closer to God.

My second belief is about our shared life on this beautiful, weary little world. I do not believe that Kevin's cancer was willed by God. It was just one of the consequences of living in an imperfect world. Someday, because a great many people will have dedicated their lives to it, a cure for cancer will be found. And many of the other ills that we suffer from may also be cured because people care enough to do the tedious work of research, of peace-making, of building community, of lending a helping hand, and of applying band aids and kisses to broken bodies and hearts.

Kevin was one of those people who made the world a better place. He enriched the lives of everyone he knew. He smiled. He loved life. He was full of joy. He was always ready to do whatever he could to make the way easier for someone else. He was a thought-full, sensitive, caring human being. He was grace under pressure, and he loved his family with every fiber of his being.

If you knew him, you know this is true. If you knew him, if you loved or cared for him, we invite you to honor his memory by doing whatever it is in your power to make life better and easier, more loving for the people within your reach, and by taking joy in every day you are given. Kevin would love that!

Many years ago we took our family to see the movie, Oh, God with John Denver in the role of Everyman and George Burns filling in as God. The one scene I have carried away from it is seeing Everyman rebuking God over all the illness, war, misery, etc. in this world and in an exasperated tone asking, "Why, if you are so powerful, why don't you do something about all this?!" God answered. "That's why I gave you each other."

Each one of you that is reading this has shared our journey, its joys and its sorrows. We know that there are literally hundreds of you whose faces we have never seen, whose names are barely known to us, as well as friends of longstanding who have shared much of life with us. God couldn't reach down and put his arms around us. Instead he brought you to accompany us, to support and comfort us, to encourage us, to cry with us. And as you shared Kevin's incredible fight to live, we know that you too were blessed.

That's why he gave us each other.

As there are no words to express deep grief, so there are no words to express profound gratitude. We can only pray that all of you will be richly rewarded in this life and in the next by the One who is the source of all goodness.

Carol and Pat

You have just read the end of Kevin's story. What follows is what it preceded it.

Some stories need to be told and I have always felt strongly that this one is in that category. It is a human story with which I believe that anyone who has ever loved deeply can identify. It is a story of courage and commitment, hope and despair, of love and loss.

Kevin was our youngest child, a delight from the moment he came into our lives. He was an extraordinarily positive and joyful person who grew into a loving and good hearted man whose life was cut short at the age of thirty-one.

It is also the story of our family and our life together both with and after Kevin. All of this has been written to memorialize for those of us who knew and loved him, his love of life and his courage in fighting to keep it. For those of you who are only meeting him for the first time, we hope that knowing Kevin will enrich your lives and encourage you to cherish those you love.

Woven throughout is also my struggle to reconcile lifelong beliefs with one of life's harsher realities.

The core of this work is built around a series of emails and journal entries that I wrote over a sixteen month period when Kevin was in treatment for cancer. Copies were kept because they provided us with a history of what was taking place.

The emails are interspersed with memories and reflections on what was happening, some of them written at the time, some in the years that followed, some now.

INTRODUCING KEVIN

We thought our family circle was complete with the birth of our fifth child. But eight years later Kevin came into our lives. We should have had an inkling of what his presence would mean from the moment he was born. With the doctor's instruction to push, Kevin came bursting into life as though shot out of a gun. My husband always said that it was a miracle the doctor hadn't dropped him!

To step back just a bit, I recall the moment we revealed to our growing family that another Farrell was on the way. We chose the time after supper. As we sat at our round kitchen table, I felt great trepidation about how they would react. After all, we were all pretty settled in. Would they welcome the newcomer or see him/her as an intruder?

There the seven of us sat:

There was Pat, husband and father of this clan, who by day proudly served as an FBI agent but by night was the fun-loving, joke-telling, teasing Irishman who loved his family above all else (except maybe playing poker).

I was a stay-at-home mom in those days, like most of the women in the 1960s and '70s. I was active in the community, but the high point of my day was dinner. It was the only time each day we were all together. I loved preparing it and looked forward to all the stories and teasing that would take place.

Kathy, fourteen, had just started high school and was a lifelong serious student. Patrick, thirteen, was the family athlete who often displayed a wry, teasing sense of humor. Bridget, twelve, our middle child, was our bright, sensitive rebel. Susan, ten, was a blond, happy girly girl who became Kevin's "other mother." Tim, eight, loved sports and reading and became Kevin's best buddy and protector.

What a relief it was when we finally shared our news: the table erupted in excitement! It was like watching a seedpod burst open. Then they each scattered off in different directions to tell their friends.

It has always been one of my happiest memories. Whatever misgivings we may have had beforehand, they disappeared in an instant.

Kevin actually had no siblings. He had seven parents — seven people who doted on him every moment, and who loved him in all the best ways. This was our family when Kevin entered it.

My husband Pat has often said that if he could magically return for five minutes to any moment in the past, as Emily did in *Our Town*, it would be to sit again at our large round table for one of our everyday dinners with all of us present, in that kitchen, in our home with Kevin seated between Pat and me. Dinner together was the highlight of our day; the unforgettable symbol of our family's life together.

Dinner was the highlight but, almost as memorable, was the noisy game of Hide and Seek that often preceded it. Pat usually called to give us a heads up that he was on his way home. If it sounded as though he had a rough day I let the children know to give Pat some time and space in which to relax for a few minutes before dinner. If he said he was stopping at Publix to pick up some crumb buns, we knew it was going to be fun and games and everyone started thinking about where they would hide.

I am not sure how or when dinner became so central to our lives. It just sort of grew organically. The fact that, like so many other women of that time, I was a full-time homemaker was a critical aspect. I took great satisfaction and pride in creating a healthy and colorful dinner. It was also the only time of the day we were all together in a relaxed atmosphere.

We had some rules about protecting our table time: no television, no answering the phone, no gathering until everyone was present. Eat. Talk. Share the day. Tell a joke. Tease someone. Laugh. An Irishman to the core, Pat loved to tell stories, make us laugh, tease more than a bit. We experienced much light-heartedness over the years around that table.

There were times when our sons were on sports teams that practiced through our dinner hour. If waiting would have delayed dinner too much, I would sit with one of them as he later devoured his warmed-over supper. No one ever ate alone.

Over the years we used dinnertime to tamp down the stream-of-consciousness chatter that came from the more verbal among us, and found ways to elicit participation from the others. As the children grew older and proclaimed any fact that seemed dubious, Pat challenged them with "What is your authority?" and they would have to leave the table and consult our encyclopedias or dictionary to support their point. In addition, since Pat and I espoused different political philosophies, the children regularly witnessed spirited debates. They did not grow up thinking there was only one way of seeing the world. That alone is an education worth its weight in gold.

As Pat and I look back on all those hours around the table, we are convinced that was the time and the place where we created our intense sensibility of being a family. Those hours at that table bonded us together into a cohesive unit: the Farrells. Even after all these years, sharing a meal around the table — any table — is still our favorite activity.

Two strong memories from Kevin at about the age of four showcase different aspects of the adult he would become.

We had very recently returned from a weeklong Florida vacation. A part of it had been spent visiting Pat's parents, aunts and uncles who lived in the Clearwater area. Bingo, swimming, candy, and being indulged by adults eager to spoil can create lifetime memories. The experiences of that week were still very fresh in all our minds when we received word that Uncle Bill's beloved wife, Helen, had quite unexpectedly died. As I tucked Kevin into bed that night and he said his prayers I realized he seemed sad. When I asked him about it I was stunned to hear him say "I feel so bad for Uncle Bill. He must feel so lonely."

I had not realized that someone so young could put himself into the heart of an adult and feel so much compassion and empathy. Those qualities became lifelong hallmarks of his responses to those around him.

In an entirely different, happier vein: We had a large circle of friends and we entertained each other with celebrations on every occasion. On one of those nights when we hosted, we had settled Kevin in our bedroom to watch television. At some point he wandered into the kitchen and asked for some ginger ale. Pat poured some into a glass for him. As he crossed the living room and turned the corner into the hallway toward our bedroom, we heard the shattering of glass on the terrazzo floor. Pat sprinted toward the noise ready to chastise Kevin who greeted him saying, "You should know I am too little to have a real glass!"

It's hard to keep your composure and reprimand a child who turns the tables on you that quickly and cleverly! That devilish quality, too, persisted.

Before Kevin, we spent most of our family vacations driving from Florida to visit our families in Ohio and Indiana. It became apparent that if we had any hopes for seeing other parts of our great country, we were going to have to make some changes. With our sixth child on the way, we would now definitely need two hotel rooms, and that was decidedly beyond our budget.

That's how we came to be campers.

We had once borrowed a pop-up camper from friends for a weekend getaway. We decided that both economically and size-wise this was the right choice for us. It fit our budget, kept us (me!) from having to sleep on the ground, gave us ample room and allowed us the freedom to explore new places we were aching to see. It was the beginning of the adventure seeking that has endured a lifetime.

I am not sure if you would call us brave or foolish, but we decided our first trip would be four weeks long. Our main destination was Yellowstone National Park, with a stop beforehand in the Tetons, and one afterward in California to meet up with seldom-seen relatives. We decided that Kevin, who would be only four months old, would be much easier to travel with at this stage than he would as a toddler a year later. We even invited Richard, our son Patrick's best friend, to join us. Whatever were we thinking! Our friends thought we had lost our minds.

Off we went in our Mercury station wagon: two adults, four teens, two grade-schoolers and an infant. We were towing a camper emblazoned with the motto "California or bust!" We drove off with Pat and me in the front with one of the children between us; either Kathy, Bridget, Susan or Tim in the back seat (tiny bottoms all); Kevin on a mattressed "shelf" behind that seat, and Patrick and Richard facing each other on seats at the very back. I think we may have exceeded the legal seating capacity!

I can assure you that tight quarters create some interesting activities. There are no issues early in the day when everyone is still groggy and napping. But as the day wears on and the days of driving accumulate, creative ways to pass the time began multiplying. Reading was always a staple, and card playing was another of the more normal pastimes.

Later in the afternoon the natives grew restless and someone would usually challenge the nearest sibling to an "ear pinching contest".

For this contest, the two participants would face each other and place a thumb and forefinger on the plump bottom of one of the other's ears and begin to squeeze it. It appears there are not many nerve endings in that part of our anatomy, but sooner or later there is pain and someone hollers "Uncle!" A rematch using the unused earlobes often ensued. Desperate times necessitate desperate measures!

All of this creativity usually meant we had had enough driving for the day and needed to set up camp. We soon learned that the primary rule was that no one could wander off — not even to use the restroom — until the camper was cranked up and the gear all put in place. Then off they went.

As Floridians and novices at camping, we realized as we reached Rocky Mountain National Park that we were woefully unprepared. Not knowing what we didn't know, I had brought along a number of quilts and blankets feeling sure they would keep us warm. We shivered almost every night trying mightily to keep the blankets close to our goose-bumped bodies. In time, as we chatted with other campers, we learned they kept warm and snug because they had sleeping bags!

One of the activities we all loved was sitting around a campfire as the day drew to a close. Nothing symbolizes the outdoors like a blazing campfire. There was color and there was heat, and we were drawn to circle around to appreciate both of those things and each other. Kevin grew to be the main builder and tender of the fire, gathering the wood, fanning the embers into flames.

Over the years we were able to gather our resources and our children four or five other times to savor the beauty of our national parks. In time, we came to the conclusion that the camper was the one of the very best investments we had ever made, second only to our home.

The ending of our days gradually evolved into an echoing of good-nights. One of the popular TV series of the time was *The Waltons*. Each show ended a with a nighttime picture of their country home, windows at first dimly lit, lights gradually extinguishing, and hearing their voices bring the day to a close. Imitating them, our camping day ended as we all settled into our sleeping bags for the night with "Good night, Mom… good night, Dad … good night … good night …" until the last one trailed off into the dark and silence of the night.

LOVE WILL MAKE THEM STRONGER

"Hey, Mom! I'm home." I could hear Kevin's voice full of his usual enthusiasm and *joie de vivre*.

"I'm up here, Kev." I was on my bed propped up on pillows resting for a few minutes before dinner. Kevin came bounding up the stairs and into the bedroom and, with the energy of the eight year old he was, bounced onto the bed and gave me a kiss.

"How was the Cub Scout meeting, Sport?"

"Great! Do you know that we are going to make cars to race in the Pinewood Derby? And you parents are not allowed to really help us. You can only supervise. It's going to be in two months. Oh, gosh, I almost forgot to tell you that I got picked as the Student of the Month. Wow, today was a really fun day!"

I grabbed Kevin and hugged him. "You are my Student of Every Month!" and both of us laughed.

"I've had a pretty good day myself," I told him "and tonight I am going out to speak to a group of parents." Responding to an impulse I asked, "Is there anything special you think I ought to tell them?"

Kevin's face grew uncharacteristically serious. It seemed he didn't even take any time to think about my question and began right in with "Parents should love their children a lot." Without pausing for a breath he went on "but they shouldn't spoil them by, for instance, buying them a toy every time they go shopping and ask for a toy." He must have questioned the wisdom of what he had just said because he hurriedly added "It's all right to buy something small once in a while!" He was warming to the topic and, thoughtful again, continued with "Once a child is spoiled he stays spoiled and then he can't be a very good parent."

Enjoying his moment at the podium, Kevin was really getting cranked up. He continued with "When parents ask children to do their chores, they shouldn't do it this way." His brows knit together and his voice deepened and took on an impatient, angry tone as he barked, "Joey, empty the wastebaskets!" Reverting back to his own voice he said, "It would be much better to speak softly and ask kindly."

His final admonition for parents was: "Remember that any child might tell one lie or take one roll of candy but he should be forgiven and spoken to lovingly because everyone has to make one mistake in their lifetime." A smile crept over my face.

But he wasn't quite finished. "At the end you have to say, 'I love you.'"

I wasn't sure what he meant. "Do you mean I should tell the parents that you love them?" I queried.

Kevin sat up on his knees and looked at me very seriously. He was clear and definite. "No, you have to tell them that *you* love them, Mom, because you know how it is: *Its love that will make them stronger.*"

MIRACLE AT RUEDI RESERVOIR

"Kevin's in trouble!" said my husband Pat as he sat bolt upright in our camper bed. We had just lain down for an afternoon nap twenty minutes earlier. He was up on his feet moving purposefully toward the door.

We were camping at Ruedi Reservoir in Colorado. It was the kind of setting that Floridians dream about: breathtakingly beautiful mountains, tall trees, cool dry air. Earlier in the day we had listened to the laughter of our daughters Kathy and Susan echoing around us as they jogged a nearby hill. Their laughter had the sound of chimes, light and shimmering. Kathy's son Charles, just eighteen months old, was on his first camping adventure and we all chuckled as his well-padded bottom would hit the ground and he would reach up for help rather than touch the dirt to push himself up. It was a purely perfect, beautiful day — until Pat sounded his alarm.

Pat is a no-nonsense realist, a let's-deal-with-the-facts kind of guy who has always provided much needed ballast for my emotional response to situations. He is not given to interpreting dreams or responding to intuition, but his urgency seemed ridiculous to me. "Don't be silly," I said and rolled over. Undeterred he left the camper saying he was going to look for Kevin.

The possibility that Kevin was in danger seemed totally unrealistic. None of it made any sense. Kevin was twelve at the time and we had given him permission, for the first time, to go off for an hour by himself. We didn't feel any trepidation in allowing him to explore the surroundings. He had plenty of camping experience although it had always been in the company of someone in the family because we usually did things together.

Impossibility and improbability often enough morph into reality. As it turned out, Kevin *was* in danger.

We have no answers for the many mysteries here, including why Pat left the campground and moved in the direction that he did. He began calling Kevin's name, and within about ten minutes Kevin's voice answered his call. Pat looked down and spied Kevin on a sharply angled cliff that looked to be about fifty feet above a "bottom." He was perched on a small outcropping, his body leaning into the chalky, clay-like soil with no other footing in reach, unable to negotiate either up or down.

Pat yelled to Kevin that he needed time to catch his breath and to think about what to do. A few minutes later, a teen came within shouting distance and Pat asked him to go to the campground and tell our son Patrick that he was needed.

Pat must have climbed the same hill that Kevin had, not easy but doable. As we learned later, when Kevin moved further along the top of the cliff he decided that he had to step around some small shrubs and bushes. As he moved precariously on the outside of them he lost his footing and slid down about ten-to-fifteen feet, landing on the "bump" of earth that arrested his slide. Pat found him there, afraid of falling further, and unable to move.

Pat and Patrick decided that their best bet was to get some rope to pull Kevin up. Luckily there was a road nearby that lead to the marina, and Patrick was able to stop someone hauling a boat that had a good length of sturdy rope on board. A knot was formed in the rope and lowered to Kevin. He inserted one hand into the loop and placed his other on the rope and was pulled to safety by the three men at the top of the cliff.

Almost the first things Pat did after Kevin was hauled up and hugged were to speak to him about the need to always remain cool and to consider how he could have helped himself. He pointed out to Kevin that he had a knife on his belt that could possibly have been used to dig into the clay to inch himself upwards.

On a lighter note, we observed that Kevin was wearing camouflage clothing that could have made it more difficult for anyone to see him. From now on his instructions were to wear red!

As they returned to the camper and recounted the adventure that could have been a tragedy, the usual afternoon storm announced itself with a clap of thunder, and the rain began to pelt our camper.

We began to wonder what would have happened ... if Pat had not responded so strongly to his unexplainable intuition ... if Pat had not found Kevin before the storm drove through the area ... if Kevin had lost his footing on the wet, slippery clay and fallen ... if the boater with his rope had not come by. The ending to this misadventure might have been quite different.

Since that time, we have wondered if Kevin had cheated death that day and if we had been given almost twenty more years with him that we might not have had.

Recently we came across the travel journal that I kept during that trip and were surprised that Kevin had added his thoughts about his experience:

I had gone hiking by myself around 5:30 PM. I went up by some cliffs and decided to climb along a ledge. I slipped and started to slide. After doing so several times, each time falling about 3 feet, I found myself 50 feet from the ground. It was a helpless feeling for I did not know what to do. I yelled for help and also Pat's name since he had been outside when I had left. After that I began to cry, for I was afraid I might die. I also prayed and asked God to help me. After 10 minutes of this my Dad came and soon after that my brother and some other people. Soon they found someone with rope and I was pulled up. After 20 minutes of hanging there I was safe and boy was I relieved.

Our son Patrick has always felt strongly that Kevin's good fortune that day was perhaps miraculous; that his death was averted by something extra-ordinary. He had a near-death experience that day but eventually, at 31, a truly tragic death.

Kevin's death shook us all deeply. "How could this happen?" He was such a vital person, with such a strong life force. It was so unfair! In some visceral way we felt a little betrayed by God.

Patrick wondered if all those years back then it could have been that God had bargained with us, and said "I will give you another 19 or 20 years with him but another tragedy will then take him. I can save him for you for awhile. He will have a chance to grow up, to fall in love and marry, experience life more deeply, more fully. I can do that — but you will not remember this bargain — and you will be angry."

Would we have taken that bargain? YES.

Perhaps if we could have remembered, we wouldn't have seen his death as the tragedy it was, but as a gift of twenty years.

I WOULD BE GLAD TO

In the daily hubbub of family life, there is much that goes unnoticed. But there are some things that are written on our hearts.

Kevin had always been a most loving and sensitive child. When he was in kindergarten his teacher was Mrs. Ruth Halden, a sweet and loving woman. One of the things she used to say to her class was: "You are my Number One," meaning that they were the most important people to her. Each of the children basked in her love.

Somewhere along the way that year, Kevin started saying, "You are my Number One, Mom." It made me feel very special and a little embarrassed because I knew how many other people loved him, too. But I never asked him to stop.

By the time Kev was a teenager, his sisters had all married and it was a decidedly quieter household without all the girlish chatter (and fighting over clothes!). With his brothers involved in sports and college life, Kevin was often the only one around and available to help with the household chores.

After a while I realized that whenever I made a request, he had a standard reply. If I said, "Kevin, turn the stereo down!" or "Kevin, could you help me carry these clothes upstairs?" or "Kevin, please sweep down the patio," his answer was always "I would be glad to, Mom." I *never* remember asking him to do anything during his teenage years that he did not answer, "I would be glad to, Mom." Five teenagers had preceded him and I knew that was not typical teenage talk. I do know that his response didn't just happen. It came about because he had thought about it and had *decided* that he would respond that way. It was a choice he made, early evidence of a lifelong habit of thoughtful choices.

Over the years I have passed this story on to our grandchildren, encouraging them to follow Kevin's example. From their rolled-eye responses I would say they doubt my memory.

His brothers and sisters were simply relieved they had not followed him in the birth order.

SATURDAY MORNINGS

Competitiveness, lots of it. Bikers, bearing down on each other. Runners, muscles cramping. Walkers, strollers in hand. Hot, sweaty bodies. Water, cool water. Chatter, lots of it. Finally, breakfast. That was our Saturday morning for a number of years.

Our family extended over a range of ages: newborns, toddlers, teens, and adults of various degrees of youthfulness. There was a place for each of us on Saturday mornings when we gathered at Kathy and Syd's home. We were there because it had the advantage of a large, nearby circle with little traffic. It lent itself to our competitive and social activities, as did a swimming pool into which exhausted parched weekend athletes could fall and be refreshed.

Bragging rights shifted from week to week. The most serious contenders were the bikers who fought for advantage on every turn, each maneuver calculated to outdo the nearest foe. Runners were focused but much more relaxed and usually used the time to exchange tidbits of chatter along the way when they were within speaking distance. It was the walkers — moms pushing strollers or holding toddlers by the hand — who got caught up on all the family news.

At the end, Florida's heat got to us all and we sat around the pool in puddles of perspiration, consuming icy pitchers full of Gatorade.

It took a while to get everyone cooled down and cleaned up but the morning always closed with breakfast at a nearby eatery. It took a while to find restaurants that welcomed a group that could vary from twelve to twenty. Our favorite place was Corky's. It wasn't exactly like "Cheers" — where everybody knew your name — but we had the same waitress, Blondie, week after week and she could have put in our orders without even asking because she came to know us so well.

After our orders were placed, Kevin usually took the youngest family members outside for a walk so their parents could have a little respite and enjoy some adult conversation while waiting for their breakfasts to be served. Satisfied with the exertion of the morning, our bellies filled with tasty food prepared by others, we each headed for home and the almost best part of the day: naptime.

FAMOUS? OR INFAMOUS?

Kevin was about to begin his freshman year at Virginia Tech. We had spent the day moving all of his belongings into the dorm. The day now at its end, exhausted, we lingered over our dinner. Our time together was drawing to a close. His childhood had ended. His life apart from us was at its beginning.

As we sat there I was trying to think of something memorable to say to him, something that would get him off to a good start, feeling confident. Then I knew, I remembered, what it was I needed to tell him.

Pat and I had been involved over a number of years in a church program called Marriage Encounter. At the end of one of the weekends on which we had served as a team, a young psychologist came up to us and said that he had a very strong feeling that one of our children was going to be famous. I responded to him, "You mean infamous!" We all laughed.

When Pat and I returned home that evening we repeated the story to our family. They were all excited about it and each one wondered if he or she was going to be the famous one. We really didn't have any idea if there was anything to this rather heart-warming prediction and tucked it away.

Now it came to mind. So I reminded him of the story and said that I believed that he was the one who would be famous.

Well, that was just the right thing to say! He sat up straight and smiled from ear to ear. I could see him taking it all in, sure that it was going to happen. He was the center of attention in our family, so it just seemed natural to him that being famous on a larger scale was entirely possible and likely.

Mission accomplished!

THE RETURN ADDRESS

His first letter to us came from Sebring, Florida, where he was spending two weeks at the YMCA camp. It was the summer of 1984. Red-haired, freckle faced Kevin was ten years old and this was his first experience of being away from the family. Since he was by eight years the youngest of our six children, you might imagine that he was spoiled rotten. That wouldn't be quite true. What was true was that his siblings indulged him and included him in almost all of their activities and he was accustomed to being with one, some, or all of them most of the time. In retrospect, we could see that being at camp for two whole weeks seemed to him much more like punishment than an exciting adventure, at least judging from his letters.

Our first clue to his state of mind came in the return address corner. Neatly penned in the corner of the addressed and stamped envelopes we had provided him was a single line: "Little Red." He sounded small and lonely, and his letter confirmed our fears. *"I've been real homesick these last few days. As a madder (sic) of fact I almost called home yesterday to ask if you would pick me up…. Mom, I would like for you to pray for me that I can stop being homesick because I feel real homesick. Thank you. Also pray for me that I'm safe here. Thank you."* What had we done to our baby!

We received three letters during those two weeks, all signed "Little Red". Although he enjoyed many of the activities, he never stopped telling us how homesick he was and to be sure to pick him up on time. Kevin was the most agreeable child, but any time afterward that I would teasingly tell him about another great camp I had heard about, he wouldn't let me finish the sentence. He was done with camp.

The next letter we received from Kevin came in 1991 from Blacksburg, Virginia where he was a student. The tenor of this letter was entirely different. The return addressed changed too. There in the corner Kevin wrote his full name and address: "Kevin Farrell, Vawter Hall, Virginia Tech, Blacksburg, VA." He sounded grown-up and confident, and his closing paragraph confirmed that view: *"On a scale of 1 to 10, the VT experience has been a 9. I feel that I have made the right decision for the interests I have. Thanks for your support, Mom and Dad, and I'm looking forward to Thanksgiving!!"* His letters from Tech always brimmed with enthusiasm for the classes, the sports and, of course, the pretty girls.

One of Kevin's requirements for his engineering degree was a year's internship. His was with a large national company and it required him to live in a small town in Tennessee for most of 1993. Now the return address was simply "Joe Engineer." His opening paragraph read: *"Well, I'm finally settled into life in this little hick town ... and I like it. Actually, it's probably more like I enjoy the freedoms, money and friendships. What a great experience this has been."* His year there was a great learning experience on many counts and he reveled in them all.

By the second semester in his internship, it was clear Kevin needed a car. Over the Christmas holiday we shopped for a used car that would get him up to and around Tennessee. We received a letter from him soon after he drove it back to Tennessee. This time the return address was: "Mr. K. Farrell". Hmm, I thought, that's rather formal. But once I opened the letter I understood: inside was the check he had written to cover the insurance on the car. He was an adult now.

On Valentine's Day in 1996 I received a card from Kevin. The return address carried the message every parent of a college student wants to receive. This card came from "The Graduate". Graduation was still three months away but there wasn't any doubt about his status. Part of his message inside was: *"You didn't think I would forget the first woman to love me, did you?!.... You have brought me to mountaintops and babbling brooks, from the dinner table to God's table, Miami to Blacksburg, diapers to boxers, from Kindergarten Kid to engineering wiz, and many places in between. I look forward to*

*celebrating many more of the joys of life with you and
Dad come May ....*"

Soon after graduation Kevin returned to South
Florida and settled in West Palm Beach. Within two
years he married his college sweetheart. We saw a
lot of him in those days so letters became
unnecessary. A few years later in 2002, Kevin and
Kathleen were blessed with a son. When my next
birthday card arrived the neatly penned return
address read "The Farrells."

Whoever would have thought that the unfolding of
a life could be captured by a single line in the return
address corner of an envelope?

KEVIN THE ENGINEER

T his anecdote about Kevin's early professional days surfaced as I probed the family for their memories. Steve, Sue's husband and co-worker at Motorola with Kevin, shared this memory:

This little story emphasizes Kevin's determination ... the details have faded over time but here it is ....

It is common at Motorola to have brainstorming sessions on a project that you are working on in order to discuss and gather ideas from other people. Usually there will be engineers present from several levels of experience. At one particular session, both Kevin and I were present. Keep in mind Kevin had been working at Motorola for a little over one year, and thus, was one of the junior engineers.

During the course of the meeting, Kevin proposed an idea as a possible solution. It was quickly shot down by one of the senior engineers. Keep in mind, this is usually a "no-no" in brainstorming sessions as all ideas are welcomed and considered. Rather than giving up, Kevin was persistent in getting his idea considered. He countered with additional reasons why his idea might work. Other engineers started to agree with Kevin and provided their support to the rookie. The senior engineer reversed his rejection of Kevin's idea and added it to the list.

Although Kevin's idea was not the final solution, he did earn a lot of respect from all those in the room that day, and future days to come.

KEVIN TO ANDERS

Kevin was not much of a writer. We have very few letters or emails from him during his post-college years. He preferred face-to-face or phone communication. However, in the fall of 2001, our oldest grandchild Anders, who was just eight years younger than Kevin, was struggling. He was having a difficult time in college and in life. Kevin reached out to Anders by sending him a Bible with the following note inscribed on the opening page:

Anders,
Prayer helps to comfort and guide me in the trying times when I am lonely, when I am sad, when I am confused ... I say a little prayer and I am comforted to know God is there. Conversely, when I feel life is going great, I give a little prayer of thanks and I feel better.

Often a Bible offers one a way to pray and to learn. I especially like Proverbs because it is very practical and easy to read. The last page of the Bible also has "Promises from the Bible," which offers certain topics that may be of interest to you.

Whether you read this Bible or not, remember that God Loves You!!

And that I love you too!

You are in my prayers,

Kevin

✉ *Email from Kevin: January 22, 2002*

I thought this was nice. Have a good day.

Kevin

Wonders of the world from a child's eyes:

A group of geography students studied the Wonders of the World. At the end of that section, the students were asked to list what they considered to be the Seven Wonders of the World. Though there was some disagreement, the following got the most votes:

1. *Egypt's Great Pyramids*
2. *Taj Mahal*
3. *Grand Canyon*
4. *Panama Canal*
5. *Empire State Building*
6. *St. Peter's Basilica*
7. *China's Great Wall*

While gathering the votes, the teacher noted that one student, a quiet girl, hadn't turned in her paper yet. So she asked the girl if she was having trouble with the list. The quiet girl replied, "Yes, a little. I couldn't quite make up my mind because there were so many."

The teacher said, "Well, tell us what you have and maybe we can help." The girl hesitated and then read: I think the Seven Wonders of the World are:

1. *To touch*
2. *To taste*
3. *To see*
4. *To hear*

She hesitated a little and then

5. *To run*
6. *To laugh*
7. *To love.*

—*Author Unknown*

(Strictly speaking, this wasn't Kevin's list, but it could have been.)

FAMILY UPDATE

Kevin was the last of our children to marry but not by much. He had warned his brothers who were delaying trips to the altar that he was going to beat both of them if they didn't move a bit faster.

Once Kevin settled down with Kathleen, our family was set. We felt a sense of completion. He was now thirty, an engineer with two advanced degrees, a husband and a father to an almost one-year-old son, with a daughter on the way.

Here was how the rest of the family looked in 2003:

Kathy, our most passionate-about-life child and a voracious learner, was married to Syd, a lighthearted, happy man with a photographic memory and a love of heated discussions. They had three children and by now had brought them almost all the way though the perilous teen years.

Patrick, our most organized and focused child, the go-to-person in our family, was married to Lisa, an enthusiastic student and practitioner of lifelong learning. Their two children were in grade school.

Bridget, who was our quickest study with the least effort, had married and divorced. As a couple, she and Andy had raised a now college-age son.

Susan, sweet, warm-hearted and intelligent, had married Steve, a quiet, gifted man who had somehow managed to adjust to our boisterous family. Together they nurtured four children who at this point spanned the ages from nine to fourteen.

Tim, who had been a terrible tempered two year old, and who for eight years had occupied the enviable spot as our baby, was now a caring, hard-working adult. His soul mate, Marie, mother to their three children who were between the ages of five and ten, has never looked at them without a smile on her face.

SERENITY S-H-A-T-T-E-R-E-D

We were camping in the luxuriant splendor of spring along the Georgia coast. It was midweek and I had been relaxing in our newly acquired motor home, lying on the couch, looking out the window into the sunny afternoon reflecting on how good life was. All I could think was, "I am so blessed."

In the midst of all this pleasure Kevin called. It felt so good "to hear his voice and his happiness" as I wrote later that night in my travel journal. Then there was a call from Tim and Marie who were making plans to visit her family in Canada later that summer. I ended my journal entry with "It's been a perfectly lovely day. The weather here has been 'gently cool' — couldn't ask for better."

I can hardly recall any days that have been more filled with beauty and a feeling of serenity and contentment.

Then it all changed. A few days later we were on our way to do some grocery shopping when we received a call from Kevin. After a while he told us he had some medical problems: "lumps and bumps" on his head and his face, and swollen testicles. A sonogram and biopsy had been scheduled. We were dumbstruck.

We sat trying to absorb all Kevin had told us and then called him back with an endless string of questions and things to consider. It seemed obvious to us that these "lumps and bumps" were surely his lymph glands and couldn't believe that any doctor would not have immediately come to the same conclusion and pursued tests months ago when they first appeared.

Later that evening Pat and I were struggling to absorb what we had heard from Kevin, and he said "I can handle any kind of problem — like the tire going on the RV yesterday. But I couldn't handle anything happening to Kevin." And the rims of his eyes reddened.

"All of this is unthinkable," I noted in my journal.

Email of May 7, 2003

Dear Friends,

As you have supported us in other difficult moments, we come to you again asking urgently for your prayers. We just learned on Sunday that Kevin, our youngest child, just 30, has been developing some lumps/bumps on his skull and down his neck. Over the last three months they have increased in size and number. In the last month his testicles have also swollen. Although he was seeing his doctors, his primary and his dermatologist, both said they had not seen anything like the lumps before. I am not sure of the sequence of all these events exactly but last week an x-ray revealed inflamed nodes around his heart. At any rate, he only told us about his medical problems this past Sunday. He is undergoing a number of tests: CT scans, x-rays, and a biopsy of one of the nodes today; also an echocardiogram, etc. As you can see, this is a very serious situation. The primary possibilities are testicular cancer or lymphoma.

So we are asking for your prayers. (I would add that Kevin and Kathleen's son Connor will celebrate his first birthday next month and they are expecting another child at the end of November.) Pray for a clear diagnosis so that treatment can begin. Pray for competent, caring doctors and other caregivers. Pray for wholeness for Kevin, for a calm and deep faith for Kevin and Kathleen and all of us who love him. Be positive in your thoughts and expect good results.

We expect to learn something as a result of today's biopsy. We will keep you up to date on what is taking place.

We are grateful that you are there for us, joining in our prayers for this most beloved child.

Carol and Pat

LIFELINES

There is a saying that "there are no atheists in foxholes." I believe it. I am here to add to that observation: "There are no atheists in the homes of cancer patients either."

Faced with life-threatening situations, we grab at any and every potential lifeline: penicillin, prayer, a floating log, a helicopter. It all depends on what is available. For us, it was medical remedies, friends and prayer.

The family members of adult loved ones suffering with any serious health issue serve only on the periphery. Important decisions are always in the hands of the patient and the patient's spouse or partner. That is a difficult place to be when the patient is your youngest child, your baby — even if he or she is in their thirties. It is very difficult to stand to the side. Parents of adult children may have input but they don't have "say". And that is how it should be, even if it is frustrating.

There are an endless number of important ways that family members and friends can help: baby-sitting, meal making, grocery shopping, covering expenses, making calls, writing notes, research, childcare, donating blood, listening. But the primary roles that I assumed were as chief communicator and asker-of-prayers.

We had developed a large community of friends over the years and we did our best to keep in touch with them. Most of those friendships had been formed around our church and its activities. As soon as it was clear that Kevin's life was in danger, we started sending out emails and begging for prayers. You will read a lot about praying in the pages to come. It was the only thing we could *do* to relieve the terrible sense of helplessness that haunted us.

We could pray and we could ask our friends to pray. And hope for a medical miracle.

Each of us must choose the lifeline that makes the most sense to us.

Email of May 10, 2003

Dear Friends,

*We now have a diagnosis on Kevin's illness: a non-Hodgkin's lymphoma, specifically it is **T-cell lymphoblastic lymphoma/leukemia. It is a very aggressive disease** usually associated with AIDS and other immune diseases. It has happened extremely fast. His first symptoms occurred about three months ago but, of course, it was not particularly alarming at that time. On Wednesday a lymph node was biopsied and he was admitted to the hospital immediately. The specific diagnosis came in on Friday, with much refinement of testing still to be done.*

The seriousness of all of this is reflected in the chemotherapy which we have been told will be "intensive, aggressive and prolonged." Kevin will begin chemo on Monday. He is expected to be in the hospital receiving chemo relatively continuously for four to five weeks and can expect to be unable to work for "months". This timeframe of treatment is only the first of six phases but the most challenging and decisive. Lymph nodes throughout his system seem to be affected and the cancer also shows in his bone marrow.

We all realize what we are dealing with but the doctors encourage us that it is "treatable and curable". Kathleen is absolutely positive that there is nothing but a good outcome to be expected. We want to share her positiveness. So we ask you to support Kevin with your prayers for wholeness, for a complete and quick recovery, for extraordinary competence for his doctors. Kevin began steroid treatments this morning for a reduction of the tumors. We are hoping this will give a good kick start to the treatment.

We visited him this morning and he looked wonderful. If it were not for all the tubes and bandages it would be hard to believe that there was anything wrong with him. His youth and healthy lifestyle are all bonuses for him.

We are trying to keep well balanced ourselves. The earlier in the day, the better things seem. The nights are the worst, especially for Kevin. The other day he said that all that mattered was that he lived, for his children; that whatever was ahead he could handle. Children are a gift, above all because they are life giving.

With deep gratitude for your prayers and support,

Carol and Pat

Email of May 15, 2003

Dear Friends,

At 6 pm last night we put Kevin and Kathleen on the plane for Houston. At 8:30 this morning he began a day of testing at MD Anderson Cancer Center there. At the end of the *day, our hope is that he will be admitted. If he is, he will be there for four or five weeks, the first phase of his treatment.*

He is at this world-class facility because of the oncologist who treated him locally. The doctor wanted a second opinion from a hospital that was outstanding, would take Kevin immediately and that would accept his health insurance. The doctor made it happen and we are grateful because all of us wanted the second opinion from an institution of the highest competence.

All of this is very difficult for Kevin and Kathleen. On the emotional level, leaving behind Connor who Kevin calls "my little man" is heart wrenching because he will not be able to even see him at a distance. It also means leaving behind the great number of people who have physically surrounded them — and Kevin is a People Person of the first order. On the physical side, Kevin will be retested in every way today including another painful bone marrow test. Beyond this we know that the treatment he will receive is going to cause extreme effects.

Kevin and Kathleen both looked, and must be, exhausted. In a way, the detachment may give them some alone time that will be renewing. Of course, if Kevin is admitted, he will never be alone. Kathleen will have to return regularly to South Florida and someone of the family will be with Kevin during those times. It's ironic that with family in so many parts of the country that he should be treated where we have no one to visit and be supportive.

*Whenever someone hears the news of Kevin their response is "I don't know what to say." The conversation usually ends with "If there is **anything** I can do…" and we know that everyone means it with all their heart. The only thing that all of us can do is **pray** and I know you will. Be positive in everything you ask on Kevin's behalf. Send all your positive energy his way. Our mantra is: No Fear. And a miracle NOW!*

We have bad moments when our energy is low. Pat and I seem to take turns at being emotional. Anyone who speaks to me hears about Kev and is asked to pray for him — it doesn't matter that they are people I have never met before. And everyone responds in the most caring way that they will pray. At rock bottom, we are confident that Kevin will come through this and all of us will be strengthened in our faith.

That's it for the moment. Thank you for everything you do.

✉ *Email of May 21, 2003*

Dear Friends,

It's difficult to know where to begin. Kevin was admitted to MD Anderson Cancer Center in Houston very late on Friday night, May 16, and his chemo treatments began almost immediately. The hospital confirmed the diagnosis he had received here in West Palm: **Acute T-cell Lymphoblastic Lymphoma.** This lymphoma acts like leukemia in that it travels through a system and spreads much like it would if it travelled in the bloodstream. It is present in his bone marrow in a significant amount: 59%.

His treatment is being supervised by an outstanding doctor who has had excellent results in a clinical study published just four years ago. Kevin is now part of Phase 2. They are pulling out all the stops for Kev. In the first study two out of three participants were cured, so we have great hope.

To tell you a bit about the treatment: It is broken down into eight stages, each one lasting three to four weeks. He will be treated on both inpatient and outpatient bases. Generally he will be in the hospital for the first five days of each cycle, then as an outpatient with visits to the clinic twice a week. Much later in this schedule he may return to West Palm to receive some of his treatments there.

During the next six months, Kevin will receive radiation on his chest and testicles. He will also receive lumbar punctures to treat the fluid in his spinal column and around his brain in order to protect them from infection by the cancer. This will continue through the next six months.

Following the initial six months or so of chemo it is expected that Kevin would be in remission, meaning that there are no signs of the cancer anywhere in his body. Once in complete remission, he will begin approximately two and a *half years of maintenance treatments. All of us need to keep in mind that we realistically have a three year battle ahead of us to get Kevin completely cured.*

I have spent the last three days caring for Connor who is the most smiling, happy baby anyone could ever ask for — even when he has double ear infections, which he does. Kathleen will return late on Saturday. Pat will go out on Friday so there will be overlap. She will be in West Palm for about five days.

The best way to handle any mail to Kevin and Kathleen is to send it either to their home address or to ours. Since Kevin is cycling in and out of the hospital, it would be hard to catch up with him any other way. We will keep you posted on any changes.

With love and gratitude, Carol and Pat

Email of May 25, 2003 from Kathleen

Mom,

Could you please pass this on to everyone on your email list that has been thinking of and praying for Kevin? I would really appreciate it!

Love, Kathleen

Dear Family and Friends,

I want and need to take some time to thank each and every one of you for your prayers, good thoughts, and warm sentiments that you've sent to Mom and Dad Farrell, who have passed them on to Kevin and me over the past few weeks. Never did either of us think that at age 30, we'd be facing the greatest medical battle of our lives, not to mention the greatest fight for our growing family that we may ever know. Nor did we ever anticipate that we would grow to depend on the love, prayers, and good wishes of so many warm and generous people, many of whom I've never had the pleasure of meeting, to carry us through it all. This morning at mass, our priest spoke of the importance of God and his love in our lives. Fr. Alex said that even if the only friend that you can count as your own is God, you are truly blessed because God is Love and where God is, there is a lot of love to be had. Never have truer words been spoken, nor have they ever been so timely in our lives. Each and every one of you is evidence of that fact.

As well as conventional medicine is working to heal Kevin's body, it is through the prayers of each of you and those you've asked to pray for him, that Kevin has continued to keep his spirit healthier and stronger than ever. You are each responsible for helping us to keep the demons and the loneliness, the confusion and anger at bay, and for instead giving us the courage to turn that energy into hope, faith and strength. For all that you have done for us, thank you just does not seem to be enough but it is all that I have to give. Please know that we pray for all of you as well, in our prayers of thanksgiving for all of the great things and people that we have to celebrate despite Kevin's illness. I am confident that in time, he will be healed and it is because of your prayers and the confidence that I have in Kevin's doctors that I believe this in my heart. Thank you all again so very much; we can't fight this without you.

Love,

Kathleen

KATHLEEN

Choosing the person you intend to spend your life with is considered by many to be the most life-impacting decision we ever make.

In one of his engineering classes during his sophomore year at Virginia Tech, Kevin noticed, and seemed charmed by, a sweet, outgoing classmate by the name of Kathleen Bridget O'Brien. Soon after sharing this tidbit of college life with his father, a green-blooded grandson of the Emerald Isle, Pat said: "Marry her!" I don't think Kevin took it as an instruction but he did eventually decide to ask Kathleen to share the rest of his life with him.

Kathleen grew up in New Jersey in an extended family even more steeped in Irish life and lore than ours was. She was the oldest of three girls born to Grace and Raymond O'Brien. Her family had a rich, exuberant social life that she thrived in. But every family has its tragedies, and for the O'Briens it was the death of their husband and father when Kathleen was sixteen.

Death rearranges life for those left behind in both large and small ways. Grace, always the heart of the family, was now also its head, and she fulfilled her duties with the good humor and energy that still animates all she sets her mind to. She loves life and it shows in all her activities. Best of all, she passed that quality down to Kathleen and her sisters Robin and Heather.

Less than two years after graduation, Kevin and Kathleen were married and settled in Palm Beach County. They stayed busy building their careers through advanced studies and hard work. Grace encouraged Kathleen to pursue her certification as an engineer, knowing how critical that step would be if Kathleen ever should need to be self-sufficient — a painful lesson she had learned after her husband's death.

During those first few years they saved and eventually bought a home neatly settled on a cul-de-sac with neighbors whose roots, like Kathleen's, were in New Jersey. This was the basis of warm and lasting friendships. It had the additional benefit of being just a few blocks from Kevin's sister Susan and her husband Steve.

Inasmuch as they were occupied with their careers, studies, and settling into their new home — and inasmuch as a we lived sixty miles away — we saw less of them. Then came the birth of Connor, and too soon after, Kevin's diagnosis, which changed all that. Our lives became entwined in intimate ways and we came to know each other better than ever. It was in those weeks and months that we came to appreciate Kathleen's many strengths.

A strong will and a bright, organized mind enhanced her friendly and positive approach to life. Kathleen's smile never dimmed, even at the darkest moments. From the beginning of Kevin's treatments, they kept a journal documenting every doctor's visit, treatment and recommendation. As Kevin was admitted to MD Anderson, she organized a schedule showing when she could be with Kevin and when family members were needed to step in. She traveled between West Palm and Houston, cared for one-year-old Connor, continued to attend to her civil engineering duties and, with Kevin, made all the decisions required in his long months of treatment. All while she was pregnant.

Above all, she was positive. She was positive about everything — but above all, that the outcome would be good. We could not have wished for a more useful or priceless quality.

Early in their marriage, Kevin told us that he was sure of two things about Kathleen: that if he ever became ill that she would take good care of him (because of the example her mother had set), and that she would be an excellent mother.

He was right.

Email of June 3, 2003

Dear Family and Friends,

I am writing this from Houston where I will be with Kevin for the next 10-12 days. He and Kathleen have leased an apartment for the next six months and I will help them make that move while I am here. Obviously they have decided that this is the best place for Kevin to be treated. Pat and I couldn't be happier about their decision.

Kevin is coming to the end of his first series of treatments. Later this morning I will meet his doctor. On Thursday they will meet again and decisions about the next phase will be made. This first series is the most crucial. Kevin's tests indicate that he has made good progress. His bone marrow test is the most crucial. At the start he had a 59% infiltration of cancer cells there. His count is now down to 5%, for which we are most grateful. But it has to get below 2-3% by Thursday.

*******Therefore I am asking all of you to concentrate on praying for a bone marrow count of 0% of cancer cells on Thursday's test. This is the big one. It would preclude the necessity of a bone marrow transplant at a later date****

Pat had a great visit with Kevin here last week. And Kathleen will be able to stay at home for a little longer time. She is a real trouper — all heart and hard work.

Kevin seems much himself but he does look a little different because his hair began to fall out over the weekend and he had it all shaved off. I haven't seen this much of his head since he was a baby! But he is just as cute and lovable!

Thank you for all your notes and cards, and especially for your prayers. We know they are working in a hundred large and small ways!

Much love,

Carol

✉ *Email of June 14, 2003*

Happy Father's Day to all of you fabulous Dads out there! We are proud of each and every one of you!!

Dear Family and Friends,

I have just returned from 10 days in Houston with Kevin, the most time we have had together since he was in college, a real gift.

While I was in Houston I was able to send one note asking you to pray for the results of the most recent bone marrow test. His bone marrow had shown a 59% invasion of "blasts" (cancer cells) when he began treatment, 5% after two weeks, and is now down to 2%. The doctors call this a "remission" which in medical jargon means "cancer cells too few to count." All of that is very good news but not as definitive as I had thought. It does not mean that Kevin is out of the woods on the possibility of a bone marrow transplant eventually, but the low numbers are a definitely positive result. Thank you for your response in prayer to this specific request. God continues to work miracles both large and small.

To give you an overview of what is happening: Kevin will receive a series of eight chemo treatments, each lasting three weeks. The odd-numbered treatments are the same and require a five-day hospital stay. The even-numbered treatments are the same and require a three and a half day hospital stay. In between Kevin is out of the hospital but makes twice weekly hospital visits for checkups and is on a very precise daily drug regimen that includes a 'shot' twice a day to build up his white cells which fight infection. These shots cost $280 each!!! We thank God over and over again for Kevin's health insurance coverage!

On Thursday I accompanied Kevin for his outpatient checkup. His platelet count was very good, surprisingly high. His white cell count quite low in spite of the twice-daily injections. Kevin also has a slight cold, is experiencing constipation and some stomach upsetness. Any infection is *potentially very dangerous and would be a setback in his treatment.*

This chemo series has brought more fatigue and Kevin rests more. But while we were there we went for a long walk every day. During his hospital stay we would walk around the block with Kevin pushing his "chemo tree" with as many as eight bags of drugs. That was quite a sight! After he was back in their apartment (more about this later), we walked the neighborhood, one night for more than an hour (no 'tree' this time). Exercising to whatever extent he is able is part of his recovery....

On my way home, bad weather caused a delay for me in Charlotte. I wandered around the airport, stopping in shops just to pass the time. In a jewelry store I spoke with two very friendly saleswomen who had no other customers and encouraged me to enjoy myself. We soon fell into a conversation and, naturally, it wasn't long before they heard about Kevin. They were mothers, and so they understood my feelings, and went on to engage me in conversation. They were delightful. When I finally stood up to leave for my flight one of them said to me: "Did we help you forget for a little while?" Jeannie and Cathy will always feel like "angels" sent to restore my spirits. You can bet I will visit them the next time I pass through Charlotte's airport.

I haven't meant to go on so but I guess this writing is in some way therapeutic for me!

On Thursday evening, Kathleen returned with Connor in tow to spend the week with Kevin. I am sure it was part of a care-full plan so that Kevin could celebrate his first Father's Day with his pride and joy, his "little man", Connor.

Although there has not been a breath of complaint from Kathleen, I can only imagine how difficult all of this is for her: the caring, the flying, the making of arrangements for Connor, working two days a week, etc. Contrary to the recommended pregnancy weight gain, she has lost ten pounds but does not express any concern about herself. I am amazed at her energy and accomplishments and so very grateful for her positiveness and can-do attitude.......

We wish all of you fathers out there every blessing for the love and devotion you have lavished on your children. May God bless you abundantly on Father's Day and always.

With love and gratitude,

Carol

ANGELS IN DISGUISE

One of the beautiful unexpected outcomes of Kevin's illness was discovering how "perfect strangers" often served as angels in disguise. There were many who crossed our paths in this way, but this reflection is about two who impacted our lives beyond any way we could have hoped for.

Kevin's health had never been an issue. He was a normal child with the illnesses and accidents that are common to all children. This was different. Now his life was desperately, seriously threatened. His doctor was exploring the best medical facilities available to treat Kevin. Since we had an extended family scattered throughout the states, we were sure he would be located in a city where some of them would be present.

Only it didn't turn out that way. It was going to be MD Anderson, the outstanding medical center in Houston, where we had not a single connection. Our hearts fell. In an email to friends, I lamented that "It's ironic that with family in so many parts of the country that he should be treated where we have no one to visit and be supportive."

As it happened, although we did not have family, we were blessed with friends, specifically Marsha who lived in Boston and who had close ties in Houston. She reached out to Chris and Kitty who responded quickly and eagerly: "How do we get in touch with them? I would be happy to call them and offer dinner, time away when necessary, or anything else that they might need." And later, "We will do our best to make their time here in Houston easier."

As generous as that sounds, it was nothing in comparison with what they actually did.

To begin, they arranged to meet them at the Rice University Student Center where religious services were held on Sunday mornings. Several people in the congregation worked at MD Anderson and introduced themselves to Kevin after Mass. Then Chris and Kitty invited them to breakfast at a favorite nearby restaurant and discovered coincidences that bonded them right from the start.

Kevin had two lengthy stays in Houston, each five months long. During those months, Kitty and Chris adopted Kevin and Kathleen — and all the rest of our family as well. We became fast friends.

These two angels loved and served and nurtured them. They started by helping them settle into the apartment that would be their home for the next months. They spent hours each and every week doing what they could to be helpful but being careful not to intrude. I need to clarify that Kitty and Chris were not retirees but prime-of-life professionals who put in long hours every day in their roles as educators.

Among their activities they visited Kevin in the hospital or babysat so Kathleen could visit or have a few precious moments for herself. They picked up family members at the airport. They treated for dinners out. Among their many admirable qualities is that they were lighthearted, laughed a lot and loved life.

Their almost final act of generosity was to pack up everything that was left behind in the apartment and put it all into Kevin and Kathleen's van after they had left Houston for the last time. They then drove it to the airport where they met our son-in-law Syd, who had flown in to pick up the van and immediately begin the drive back to Florida.

How can you not love and be eternally grateful to those who love and care for your children like you would, like they were their own? Everyone in our family spent some time in Houston but Chris and Kitty were always there, ready and willing to pitch in and do whatever needed doing. There was no task they were not willing to tackle. No family member could have done more. No amount of money could have purchased all that they so lovingly accomplished out of the great goodness of their hearts.

Only angels in disguise serve that way.

FAR FROM HOME

Being treated for a serious disease in a facility far from the home you love is never ideal, but MD Anderson was the next best thing. We always felt that, under these circumstances, there was no better place to be. The hospital was a dynamic place. It seemed charged with professionalism, hope and positivity — starting with their motto: Making Cancer *History*. We felt Kevin was in good hands.

Little things mean a lot when it comes to hospitals. For one thing, each room was a private room with a Murphy bed that could be pulled down to accommodate a family member who wanted to stay overnight. Then there was the menu: you could order anything you wanted, at any time of day. Cancer doctors are not concerned about what you eat; only that you eat. There was a grand piano in the lobby. Occasionally a guest would sit down to play it. Other times a professional provided beautiful music. Music does soothe the soul. There was a room to accommodate visitors where snacks, needlepoint pieces and other diversions were available. There was a Wellness Center where classes were offered. Above all, patients were cared for by medical professionals, emphasis on *cared*. I especially remember with gratitude the lumbar puncture tech who executed this painful procedure easily if not painlessly and with a touch of good humor.

In the ten months that Kevin was in treatment at MD Anderson, there were never more than a few hours between when one family member left and another flew in. If the children could not be in Houston and needed tending in West Palm, they were always cared for in their home, most often by Grace, Kathleen's unstoppably energetic and good humored mother.

One of the things we were sure of was that Kevin and Kathleen, both engineers, were very competent. From the very beginning, they kept a notebook with every medical detail in that one place. There were no little slips of paper to be hunted down later or lost. Kathleen also organized a travel schedule, because our families were committed to being present and helpful wherever they were needed.

Not everyone with loved ones in distant hospitals is blessed with large families to call on and/or the resources to make being there happen. Or with people not just willing but eager to be present, adjusting their lives to fit whatever needs arose.

My husband Pat has a very sharp memory of being on the bus that he and Kevin often took between the housing complex and the medical center. He recalled that, while there might be as many as 15 patients on board, only two of them would usually have a companion. Fighting cancer is a battle. Doing it without physical companionship must feel like a hell.

Even in the best of hospitals.

Email of July 9, 2003

Dear Family and Friends,

Kevin met with his doctor yesterday and received the results of a number of tests which have been administered over the last two weeks — and they have all been good. Kevin is officially in remission! Again, the medical definition of remission is that 'no cancer can be seen' or 'as far as they can detect'— but we will definitely accept that with a large sigh of relief and a great prayer of gratitude.

Apparently, from what the doctor said, this is as expected at this point in the treatment. The 'trick' is to stay in remission. The two primary tests that indicate remission for Kevin are the bone marrow and CT scans of his chest, abdomen and pelvis. His bone marrow was down to 2% of the cancer cells that had been as high as 59%; the CT scans show the various lymph nodes as either reduced to normal or seriously reduced. There is still some evidence of them around his heart and they will continue to be monitored.

In no way does this alter the course of his treatment which means that he still has the remaining five series of chemo ahead of him. He will also have radiation treatments after the chemo is completed.

These results are very encouraging to us all, especially so because Kevin has had a challenging couple of weeks. We know that this healing-in-process flows from both earthly and heavenly sources. We are all deeply touched by your steadfast support. Please keep it up. Even though this is a significant milestone, Kevin still has a long haul ahead of him.

Right now Kathleen and Connor are with Kevin in Houston and it is wonderful to hear the delight that Connor brings to their lives. Every day seems to bring some new awareness or skill that expands his world — and theirs.

God bless you all!!

With love and gratitude,

Carol

Email of August 16, 2003

Dear Family and Friends,

I returned late on Thursday night from a weeklong visit with Kevin. He was in the hospital during the first two days of my visit receiving his fifth series of chemo treatment. During those days he slept a great deal and ate very little.

So it was a delight to see both his spirit and appetite return in the subsequent days. Even though the hospital is a place of healing for Kevin, he finds the days there very difficult and counts the hours until he can leave.

Before I returned to Miami I was able to accompany him on a visit with his doctor who is pleased with his progress. It was noted that in the most recent bone marrow test, no 'blasts' (cancer cells) were found. The doctor is quite hopeful that Kevin will not require a bone marrow transplant although that decision will be made later. We are relieved that although not all the tests of Kevin's siblings are complete, we know that Kathy (his 'first' sister) is a match should we need one. The doctor was also very encouraged in that Kevin's most recent CT scans were "really good — a very good response."

All in all, as that old saw goes, Kevin is in good shape for that the shape that he is in! For that we are grateful. He has been blessed to have escaped some of the chemo's worst side effects. The most troubling for him are stomach discomfort, changes in his taste buds, headaches and fatigue. We know that the treatments ahead of him will continue their debilitating course before the rehabilitation can begin. Kevin has three more series of chemo still to come; then radiation treatments. The chemo should be complete by the end of October.

Please pray that Kevin continues in remission, for all who are responsible for his care and healing, and for all the *many others who battle cancer. Pray for good health for Kathleen and their waiting-to-be-born baby.*

Thank you for your support and love and prayers, all of which are very tangible to those of us on the receiving end of them. May God bless you abundantly!

With love,

Carol

HOSPITALS

Trips to the hospital are a part of every family's experience. A quick in-and-out is the desirable way to participate in the healing services they provide.

Over the years, with six active children, we made numerous trips to the ER at our local hospital. Kevin seemed to give them more business than anyone else in the family: diving into the shallow end of a pool; placing his hand on the hot manifold of a lawn mower that had just been shut off; falling off of a bike and splitting his upper lip open; tossing a ginger ale bottle into the air and having it hit the counter where it shattered and cut a deep gash in his leg. These were just a few of his escapades.

On the way to the hospital that time, he was crying, "Why me? Why me! Why does everything happen to me!" We thoughtfully refrained from the obvious answer to his question at that point. We made such frequent trips to the ER that I thought we should have gotten some kind of "frequent patient" designation, or a discount, or that some doctor was going to say "You again, Kevin?"

As we settled in for long stays at MD Anderson, the memories of these quick in-and-out visits returned and I wondered if he was now silently asking "Why me?" again.

Knowing Kevin, I think not.

Email of September 8, 2003

Dear Family and Friends,

As some of you already know, Kevin was hospitalized on Wednesday night, September 3, because he developed a fever. Fevers are dangerous for patients receiving chemo because they indicate the presence of infection in a body which has few defenses to fight it. His doctor had informed him earlier that almost everyone has one such episode in the course of the eight series of chemo treatments. (Kevin has almost completed his sixth.) One possible source of the fever was in reaction to the blood transfusions he received earlier that day. (He has received blood on about a dozen occasions.) The other possibility was an infection from exposure to who-knows-what-source. A blood culture which took 24 hours to process was required. It turns out that he does have an infection, the name of which is beyond me.

On this Monday morning, he is still in the hospital. Each day the fever abates only to return later in the day. He is receiving powerful antibiotics which are supposed to knock out the infection. His next series of chemo cannot begin until this infection is stopped.

It is a challenge to stay focused on the positive when an illness is protracted. I find our spirits lag and then I think how much more difficult it must be for Kevin and Kathleen.

So I ask your prayers for them, for whatever their needs must be.

Pat returned last night from a week with Kevin. Kathleen and Connor arrived this morning, although she will not be able to see him since Connor may not be brought into the hospital. I will fly to Houston a week from today.

Thank you for your emails, your calls and most of all for your prayers. I must remind myself often to focus on our original thought: No fear. A miracle now.

Carol

Journal Entry September 9, 2003

It looks like our hopes and prayers are being answered. Kevin was discharged from the hospital after his fever was reduced enough to be considered within manageable levels. He has taken home with him some powerful antibiotics which he has been taught to administer to himself over five separate hours each day until next Tuesday. He is scheduled to be readmitted to the hospital for his seventh chemo series at that time.

At every big and little crisis I have to fight panic. Part of it is that I know something bad is happening and don't usually understand where it fits on the Panic Scale so everything to me is at the top. Anything that threatens to hurt someone I love is an enemy that I should be doing battle with. Another part is the feeling of helplessness: that I am on the outside looking in with my hands tied behind my back. I am used to being part of the solution.

It is so maddening to be on the outside.

Email of October 10, 2003

Dear Family and Friends,

Early in September I spent time with Kevin as he experienced his seventh series of chemo. It was one of his better hospital stays, I think because he could see that the end of his chemo treatments was in sight. He began making plans for terminating his apartment and furniture leases. He was giving some thoughtful consideration about returning to South Florida and his job and the beginning of his radiation treatments here.

Last weekend he came home to be part of our annual family weekend. Unfortunately he hardly arrived before he developed another fever along with a painfully sore throat. He was admitted to the hospital on Sunday morning. The tests that were needed to identify the source of the infection took about four days to complete. Ultimately it was decided that the triple-line port in his shoulder through which the chemo is delivered was the source of the infection. They removed it yesterday and inserted another type of port into his upper arm. His throat and tongue were so painful that he was given morphine. He is finally much improved today and should be released within the next 24 hours, returning to Houston on Monday.

I had never seen Kevin look so totally unlike himself. He has always been the liveliest, most joy-full person. To see his face creased with pain, and his eyes so blank, made me realize like nothing else has, that I really had no idea what this experience has been, and is, for him.

But it is onward now to this last chemo series, a great milestone. He is so anxious to be home and resume a somewhat normal life. The idea of work looks wonderful to him! He plans to return part-time while he is taking his radiation treatments.

These last weeks may be the most challenging yet. Of one thing we are sure: that God is good and that he will see all of us through this time. He has poured out his blessings on us through each of you, and we are grateful.

Carol and Pat

Email of October 31, 2003

To our dear family and friends,

We are on the brink of Thanksgiving. As I write those words

I wonder: Can thanks-giving ever be out-of-season? I think not.

At this time in our life, we are overwhelmed with gratitude for the blessings of this year. When I was in college I had a spiritual director who preached that with every large cross comes great blessings, and with every great blessing comes a large cross. We have lived that out this year as never before. The blessing and the cross came together in the love we have for each other.

In this moment we are celebrating Kevin's return home to Florida. His five month exile in Houston undergoing chemotherapy was a painful experience for all of us. When the life of someone we love is threatened it heightens our emotions. The lows are lower, the highs higher.

Kevin's excellent response to treatment is due to many factors: his outstanding medical care, his youth and generally healthy lifestyle were obvious physical factors. They were supported and enhanced by the prayers, the notes, cards and good wishes, the generosity and sacrifice of all of you 'out there.' Faith in the good God who loves each of us, coupled with your faith-full presence in our lives made all the good news possible.

*For all of that, we can **never thank God, or you, enough.***

Kevin's cancer was the cross. You are the blessing.

God is the constant presence, our rock of safety.

But it is not over yet. Kevin begins five weeks of radiation next week and will continue with local chemo treatments, and regular though infrequent extended care visits in Houston over the next three years.

So we continue to depend on your prayers for Kevin, for Kathleen and Connor and his soon-to-be-born sister or brother. And you thought you were off the hook!

May God bless you a hundredfold for all you have done to bring us this far!

With our love and gratitude, and prayers for you and yours,

Carol and Pat

THANKSGIVINGS OVER THE YEARS

Cherished family traditions often have unremarkable beginnings. Perhaps they come about due to unusual circumstances or a casual invitation, but seldom with intentionality. That's how it was for us when in 1977, our close friends Larry and Karen suggested that we celebrate Thanksgiving together pilgrim-style: under the sky, camping. As the time grew closer, about six other families joined us. It was a novel idea but highly doable in South Florida. And we knew just the right spot.

Highlands Hammock State Park in Sebring already had some history for us as it had served as a midway meeting point with our beloved Aunt Aggie and Uncle Levern who lived in Clearwater. We liked the tall trees that reminded us of our Northern roots. It was big, had trails and a swampy boardwalk where we could occasionally catch a glimpse of an alligator or two.

That weekend must have been a hit with those of us who gathered there because we kept coming back year after year. Whatever we were doing was contagious, because our numbers gradually increased until there were several years we numbered over two-hundred. Most of the adults knew each other from being involved in Marriage Encounter weekends. Having our children get to know each other was a big bonus.

We would set the time for dinner and lift or drag the picnic tables together into a big circle. Each family provided their own complete meal. Over time we had some scouting graduates with us who roasted their turkeys hanging from a chain in a chicken-wire and foil enclosure. Those same pioneer-type folks even baked pies in an oven made from a heavy liquor box covered in foil and fired with charcoal.

Weather is usually not too big a factor in Florida. Most weekends it was mild and sunny, but there were a few in which the cold tempted some to get too close to the campfires, and they found their sneakers smoking and their toes toasting! But wet was what we all dreaded. One year we had to hang plastic sheets from one tent to another to keep dry. Maybe that was the weekend that it also got so cold that everyone drove into town to buy hats, scarves and space heaters. I remember well that time and how Pat and Suzanne treated us to deep fried onion rings that were heavenly. Only one year were we ever displaced from the wide-open spaces to one of the park's large shelters to savor our feast.

Part of our ritual was that Aunt Aggie, Uncle Levern, Grandma and Grandpa Farrell would drive to the park from Clearwater on the day after Thanksgiving and we would celebrate Thanksgiving again. It was probably that same rainy weekend when we found about fourteen of us in our pop-up camper and I was afraid that if we didn't keep everyone evenly distributed in that small space we were going to tip the camper.

It is hard to remember exactly when certain activities began to be incorporated into the weekend, but I think that the annual football game came before any other. At first it was just a group going out into an open field, dividing up into small teams and having fun. It was serious from the beginning, but was never so serious that all the little kids didn't get a chance to carry the ball. That has remained a hallmark of the game. However, there was a time when there were so many players that we divided up into offense and defense. We had cheerleaders, usually led by Barbara strutting her stuff with turkey feathers a/k/a palm branches. For a brief time, the players were all men and boys with the women relegated to cheering — but not for long. The football game has remained part of every weekend. The only difference is that now the youngsters are making sure their elders get to carry the ball once in a while!

At some point in those early years, Bruce organized a race through the three-mile loop that went through the park. It was quickly named the

Turkey Trot. The run took place early on the morning of Thanksgiving, and our group had some friendly rivalries going on. In time, others asked if they could also run with us. Then there was the Mystery Runner who came in from Sebring for several years just at the beginning of the race. Bruce had no idea what he had started. Now the Turkey Trot is an officially sanctioned race that attracts hundreds of runners. Of course, *we* still have some of the best.

In more recent years, soccer has been added on Saturday afternoon. This is where our young folks really dominate and show up their less gifted and much slower parents. This game and the football game are usually followed by ice cream for all the players. This before-dinner-dessert is followed by Kathy and Syd's hamburger/hot dog and all-the-trimmings feast.

Nighttime, every night, finds all the "kids" playing Man Hunt. I think of it as some kind of miracle that no one has run into a tree and broken a nose as they dash around in the dark.

While the kids are pursuing each other in and out of the campsites, on Friday night another sport is taking place in our motor home: Pat's Poker Party. I wish I could videotape it. The men have so much fun needling each other. If you think women talk non-stop, you should give a listen here! I've begun going into bed early just so I can overhear the chatter and join the laughter.

A part of the weekend we all looked forward to was our version of Saturday Night Live. Many of the families prepared little skits, talent being no requirement, only guts. We laughed when the acts were funny and we laughed when things were bad. There were jokes and skits, stories and singing. But a good time was had by all. (It distresses me to say that as our numbers have shrunk we have lost this tradition.)

On one of those nights Kevin, who was about ten at the time, had a bit of fun with one of our good humored adult friends. Kevin took the stage, bent down in a position to start an imaginary lawnmower, pulling at the starter with all the appropriate sound effects. After several unsuccessful attempts he called Rich up to help him and instructed him to give it a good pull and see it he could get it going. Lo and behold, it worked, of course — and Kevin gleefully announced that he "knew it only needed a Big Jerk!"

We all will always miss Kevin who never stopped being a kid. He played a part in many of the activities of his nieces and nephews, and of their lives. He *loved* Thanksgiving. One of his — and their — favorite moments came when he would line them up and say "Open-your-mouth-and-and-let-me-see-how-much-whipped-cream-I-can-fill-it-with." They all loved Kevin.

One of the highlights of the weekend had always been when we paused and gathered to celebrate Mass. Originally it had taken place around the campfire later in the weekend. Over time, we gathered after Thanksgiving dinner and Fr. Mike Flanagan, our longtime family friend, had been the celebrant. Father Mike has gone one to his heavenly reward, but he and Thanksgiving will always be woven together in our memories.

There are times when I worry that the essence of this holy-day, of giving thanks, is forgotten. We are all so happy to have this time with our extended family for catching up on what's been happening and for experiencing so much joy. But when our turkey and all the trimmings are hot and ready to be served, we pause to express our gratitude for the endless gifts with which we know we have been blessed.

Our family continues this celebration to this day but our numbers are smaller now. Usually there will be only about fifty of us. It is our great family celebration when everyone from near and far will gather if it is humanly possible. It's just too good to miss. This is a tradition we cherish and know it will continue even as it changes.

One of the years that not everyone was present was in 2003. Kevin was now in Florida, in remission, but he and Kathleen were not camping with us. They had necessarily opted to stay at home awaiting the birth of KerryAnne who dutifully arrived the day after Thanksgiving, giving us one more reason to be thankful!

A PAUSE

From the end of October until the end of February, we all lived fairly normal lives. Kevin resumed as much of his Before Houston life as possible. His company welcomed his return on a half-day basis so that his treatments could continue. Kevin was so eager to do "normal."

All of us felt a great debt of gratitude to Motorola. They accommodated Kevin in every possible way. Most significant of all was their policy that provided employees on long-term medical leave to receive 60 percent of their salary, tax free. To deal with serious medical issues and to also worry about maintaining one's position and an income is a problem no person should ever have to face. But many do. Companies like Motorola need to be highlighted, appreciated and emulated.

During Kevin's first five weeks at home, he had daily radiation treatments to the nodes around his heart. He continued his chemo regimen locally, and occasionally made maintenance trips back to Houston.

One of the highlights of the year for our family is a party which we have hosted the weekend before Christmas for as long as I can remember. The numbers have increased because all the families have grown. And the space seems more crowded than ever because all those formerly little people have grown up into rather tall adults. But the format has been changeless: food, drinks, talking and singing. Most memorable is a very animated version of the "Twelve Days of Christmas" which is acted out with gusto. Quieter moments come as one of the grandfathers reads Clement's "The Night Before Christmas" with the smallest gathered about his knees. That is followed by a reading of Luke's account of the birth of Christ and the singing of "Silent Night." Dessert is the closer.

Kevin and Kathleen were also able to enjoy some special moments as he described in this email:

Kathleen and I had a nice time at Fr. Mike's ... On Saturday we had dinner at Sue and Steve's ... which is always interesting and fun! Relative to celebrating Valentine's Day and our anniversary ... it was very nice with cards and small fun presents. Connor gave me an especially nice card. It read: "For my daddy. You always think of fun things for us to see and do ... you're more than just my daddy — you are my favorite buddy too." I loved it.

Take care, Mom. Love, Kevin

It's pretty obvious that Kevin and Kathleen's lives could hardly have been called normal during this interim. Adjustments were being made in every direction. After all, they had just welcomed KerryAnne, a happy, smiling bundle of energy from the moment she arrived. Happiness was the order of the day. Life is a precious gift and a baby brings home that truth in an unmistakable way.

At some point during this pause Sue remembered someone commenting to Kevin that it must have been a rough year for him. His response was, "No, it was a great year. KerryAnne was born this year and I couldn't have been happier."

The rest of us were all delighted to be settled, to be "in place." We went about our daily lives grateful for the routines we usually take for granted.

Things seemed to be progressing on track.

Eight-year-old Kevin — full of life, love and mischief.

Kevin loved building and tending our campfires.

Slugger!

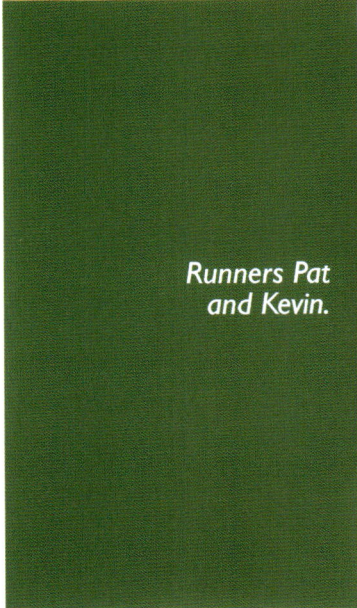

Runners Pat and Kevin.

Ann and Kevin: First high school prom.

Up a tree in Colorado with Susan and Tim.

Family photo at Greynolds Park.

Kevin, the babysitter, with Sean.

Kevin's first car. It couldn't go over 60 mph, but he loved it!

Enjoying the outdoors in Virginia. 1994.

Pat, Kevin and Carol. Virginia Tech graduation. May, 1996.

Kevin's wedding day, 1997. A little hamming it up with Tim, Pat, Anders, Brian and Charles.

Celebrating a birthday, July 2001. Back row: Tim, Kathy, Carol, Pat, Bridget. Front row: Susan, Kevin, Patrick.

Brothers ski trip 2001.

Kathleen, Kevin and Connor. Easter Sunday 2003. In the plastic egg we each received was a photo of Connor, whose t-shirt announced "Big Brother to Be in November."

Connor

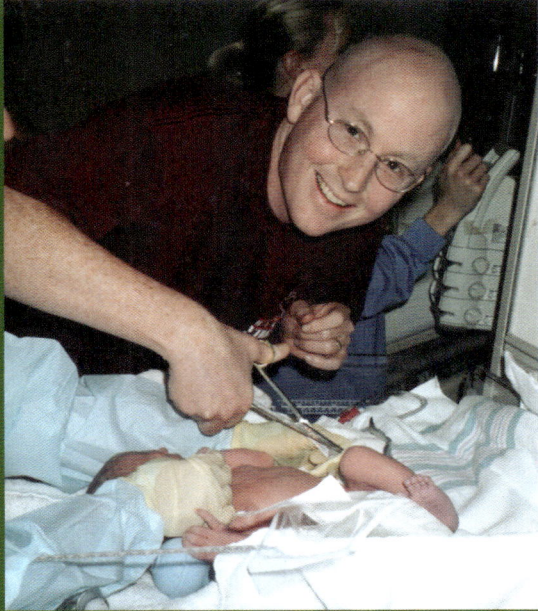

Proud dad cutting KerryAnne's cord.

Kevin with "angels" Chris and Kitty.

Brothers: Patrick, Steve, Kevin, Tim and Syd. March 16, 2004.

Kevin, Kathleen, Connor and KerryAnne. KerryAnne's baptism and Kevin's anointing, March 16, 2004

Email of March 1, 2004 11:16 PM

This request is going out to you tonight because each of you is a person of prayer. Kevin will be having CT scans on Tuesday afternoon and a biopsy of a lump on his scalp on Wednesday afternoon. He discovered the lump about ten days ago, saw his Houston doctor for a previously scheduled exam on Friday, his Florida oncologist today. Please pray in the most positive way for Kevin's health. He has been so blessed by your prayers all along this journey. We depend on them again. Still.

You can be sure that I will share the results of these tests with you just as soon as we receive them.

Carol

Email of March 4, 2004

Dear Family and Friends,

We received some very encouraging results yesterday: all of Kevin's CT scans came out "clean". We are incredibly relieved and encouraged! Any enlargement of lymph nodes there would have been devastating news. The results from yesterday's biopsy will take longer, anywhere from two days to two weeks depending on what laboratory is designated to do the testing. You will hear from us whenever we get these results.

It occurs to me that some of you may not know that the first symptoms Kevin experienced last year were the lumps on his scalp — which were swollen lymph nodes. That knowledge will help you understand why this lump seems so alarming to us.

The strong sense of being wrapped in your prayers is a source of great strength and confidence for us ….. Please continue to pray for Kevin, and for the many others in our world who suffer with life-threatening situations.

Praise God from whom all blessings flow!

Gratefully,

Carol

Email of March 11, 2004

To our dear children,

There is no easy way to pass on this news. Kevin's biopsy shows "residual signs of cancer."

He called us about 6:20 this evening. He and Kathleen had just seen the local oncologist who was in communication with Kevin's doctor at MD Anderson. Kevin will be returning to Houston soon, probably by Monday. It is highly likely that he will need a bone marrow transplant. He and Kathleen have many decisions they will have to make as they take in this latest development. It is possible that he could spend months again in Houston. Nothing has been decided.

Sending this email seemed easier than calling each of you directly. Call us if you would like to but please do **not call** Kevin tonight.

All our love,

Mom and Dad

Email of March 12, 2004

Dear Family and Friends,

This is not the news we wanted to be able to pass on to you: Kevin's tests show "residual signs of cancer" and he will be returning to MD Anderson in Houston next week. He saw his local oncologist yesterday (Thursday) afternoon when this information was given to him. It is very likely that a bone marrow transplant will be part of the plan and that his hospital stay will again be lengthy.

Many preliminary but important decisions will have to be made over this weekend. Other, more serious ones, considered next week.

We come to you again, begging prayers for Kevin: that whatever treatments are advised will be the most beneficial to him, that the treatments will be the least traumatic possible, that Kevin will be restored to full health, that all those who minister to his body and spirit will be filled with wisdom and compassion and extreme competence, that Kevin and Kathleen may be graced with courage and hope and a deep faith. We ask this in Jesus' name. Amen.

Carol and Pat

EMAILS: OUR LIFELINE

It was the emails that we sent, and received in response, during Kevin's long struggle to live that prompted this gathering of our memories. I discovered a great source of support and strength in them. A friend had suggested that if I would rather write a blog, I would not have to be "bothered" with personal responses to them. What he did not understand is that, not only was I not bothered by them, but I desperately needed them. I needed to feel that I had mustered all the strength there was available to help Kev fight his fight. I needed to read that our friends were with us, caring about each new development, sending back words of encouragement and hope, offering help and insights. There seemed to be so very little that I could do to impact his survival. But this I could do.

At first, the emails went out to our extended family in Ohio, Indiana and Colorado. Very soon I included friends from church and other groups with which we were associated. Then I reached back to people with whom we communicated only at Christmas. Of course, friends and colleagues we had made through our professional lives were part of this extended family of ours. It never made a difference that we belonged to different denominations or different faiths. It was the human factor that connected us.

Most often, my emails were composed on my home computer. A good number were generated from the computers available for use in the hallways of MD Anderson — unfamiliar computers in noisy hallways. Using them also gave us a way to use the time when we had to step out of Kevin's room. We were grateful for them.

By the time of our last emails, perhaps a hundred addresses were noted. I know that many recipients forwarded their emails to others who would care, and who would hope and pray with us. I know there were many whose names we never heard but to whom we owed gratitude. We welcomed having them disseminated as far and widely as possible.

RETURNING TO MD ANDERSON

The night before this dreaded return for medical treatment in Houston, our families gathered in Kathleen and Kevin's home for two significant rituals. The first was for the baptism of KerryAnne, which had been scheduled for a few weeks later. It seemed prudent to celebrate her official welcome into the faith now since we could not know what the future weeks held in store.

It seemed appropriate and timely to enlarge the evening by also having Kevin anointed in the sacrament of healing. Kevin looked particularly good that night. It was a solemn ceremony, full of emotion for each of us. We were all there together, gathered in strength, full of both hope and fear.

Our flight left in the afternoon of St. Patrick's Day. It seemed something of an irony for the O'Brien and Farrell families to be "celebrating" it in this way.

Actually, it was hardly celebratory. It was a wretched day in which it seemed nothing went well.

To begin with, the preparations for all of us to return to Houston were rushed. At the airport, one of our pieces of luggage exceeded the fifty-pound limit, and books and toys had to be removed on the floor at the counter and placed in other luggage. While Kevin had seemed great, almost like himself the night before, he definitely did not feel well that day.

The flight was long and late in the day and we were exhausted. When we finally made it to the car-rental agency, two infants and four adults dragging car seats and all manner of bags, we had the misfortune of being "helped" by someone who appeared to have not a speck of human decency in her body. She seemed to do everything she could to make the rental a most difficult process. One look at Kevin would have told anyone, especially anyone in a medical center city like Houston, that here was a man in great distress.

I wanted to scream.

Email of March 23, 2004

Dear Family and Friends,

I am writing this from Houston. I came here with Kevin, Kathleen, Connor, KerryAnne and Grace last Wednesday, March 17th. Kevin saw his doctor on Thursday and was admitted that night. The following day he had CT scans, a bone marrow puncture and the most unloved procedure of all, a lumbar puncture.

So much has happened I am not sure if I am repeating myself so please bear with me. Kevin's biopsy came back positive, much to our shock; the biopsy is the ultimate diagnostic test. We do know that Kevin will be receiving a bone marrow transplant, and that Kathy and Sue have both met preliminary tests as donors. They will each be taking one more test to determine ultimate eligibility.

Right now Kevin is in the hospital for five days of chemo. He will then be out for about 14 days but staying in Houston. There is some question whether he will receive another cycle of five days in, 14 out. That was what we were originally told. For the bone marrow transplant he will be in the hospital for at least a week to prepare for it. They will remove all immunity from him and begin anti-rejection drugs, I think. He will be in the hospital for a month after the transplant and then have to live within ten minutes of the hospital for the next three months.

Yesterday he received some results that really knocked the wind out of us. Last year the cancer cells/blasts in his bone marrow were at a high of 59%. Three weeks ago when he was here in Houston we were encouraged to know that the blasts were at 2%. We were dumbstruck yesterday to learn that his blasts are now at 79%. That is an incredibly high number.

As I reread what I have written, I am struck by the fact that it is so unemotional, so factual. Part of the reason is that I am writing in a noisy tech room in the hospital and am having a hard time concentrating. I guess what I feel is anxiety and fear when I am tired; hope and faith when I am in a better state; and a kind of constant feeling of stress.

The one bright spot in all of this is that I am KerryAnne's chief caregiver. As I wheel her around the hospital she brings smiles to so many faces that I know her being here is a great blessing, especially to me.

Please pray that Kevin's 'numbers' improve. That the chemo does what it is supposed to do for him. That the doctors are extremely wise in the decision they make for Kevin. That all of us can hang onto and focus mainly on the hope that this will bring Kevin a complete cure. Pray for Kevin's needs whatever they are, and for Kathleen's too.

With a heart full of gratitude,

Carol

BABY THERAPY

Dear KerryAnne,

Did you know that babies are the very best anti-wrinkle cream ever invented? It's because they make us smile so much! Whenever we look at a baby we smile, our faces soften and all the lines and wrinkles almost disappear. We feel good when we look at a baby and feeling good always improves our health. We aren't thinking of that when it happens but whether we think of it or not, it is true.

I discovered all this as I walked the halls of MD Anderson Hospital in Houston with you, KerryAnne. You were only four months old when we spent a week together while your daddy was a patient there. I had spent many hours there at other times but this was the first time that you accompanied me, or more accurately, I accompanied you *because you were clearly the center of attention.*

Normally time there was spent chatting with other family members of patients, having the coffee and cookies served up by the numerous and gracious volunteers. Sometimes I listened as another visitor or a patient sat down at the grand piano in the lobby and made beautiful music. Or I worked on a small piece of needlepoint that was offered as a mind-distracting way to pass the time. Or by reading, walking, praying or visiting the Wellness Center that offered classes that de-stress patients and family alike.

Having you there changed my experience entirely. People of every age and description would stop and look into the carriage. They would ask "How old is she?" "What is her name?" or "What beautiful eyes she has!" "She looks like a little angel!" or "Seeing her makes me miss my own grandchild!" When they continued on their way, it was impossible not to notice that they looked younger and less stressed. And as I looked at them I felt that way too.

That was a memorable week. It was so satisfying to speak to so many people who approached us with such happy faces.

The following week provided a totally different experience. You and your mom had returned to your home in Florida while I stayed behind to be with your dad. I missed you! Here I was, all alone in the waiting rooms and hallways. No one stopped me to smile. No one even seemed to notice I was there. I felt invisible!

That's when the idea of Baby Therapy came to me. Wouldn't it be wonderful to bring babies into hospital lobbies and rooms and have them work their magic by just being present? I am convinced that healing rates would go up and stress levels down. They wouldn't have to coo or laugh. They could even just be sleeping.

What do you think about this, KerryAnne?

Email of April 1, 2004

Dear Family and Friends,

Kevin has been in Houston two weeks now. Not much progress has been made as to knowing what the next steps will be — whether he will get another cycle of chemo, the likely course of action, or begin to be prepared for the bone marrow transplant. This week has not been easy for Kevin as he had to be hospitalized on Monday due to an infection in the line carrying the chemo into his system. It has been terribly stressful and frightening. His "numbers" have been off the charts, either too high or too low. I don't know if we might be more or less traumatized if we understood everything better.

Today we saw his primary doctor who explained that cancer cells have, for the first time, appeared in his spinal fluid. That was not anything we wanted to hear. In addition to the fact that it is now infecting another system, it means that he will now be subjected to two lumbar punctures a week. I don't know how Kevin copes so well. After taking it all in and being quiet for a while, he goes back to his sweet, uncomplaining way.

We will probably reach out to the Church community here in Houston to donate blood and platelets in Kevin's name, and for him very directly. Unfortunately he has a rare blood type and yesterday there was none available to transfuse him!

Each day seems to bring a new challenge.

Some personal decisions have been made: Kathleen has taken a leave of absence from her position. This Saturday she will return with Connor and KerryAnne to take up residence in Houston for the next months. An apartment and furniture have been leased. Syd, our Kathy's husband, is on his way here to Houston in Kevin and Kathleen's minivan loaded with necessary household and baby equipment. He arrives on Friday giving us just enough time to get things in place before Kathleen arrives.

The computers here in the hospital allow a limited number of email addresses to be on each email. Please direct this letter to anyone you know would usually receive it from me with apologies at not being able to do better.

I will be returning to Miami on Monday. Pat will be staying here until Easter Sunday.

We all send our thanks for your prayerful support of Kevin and all of us at this time. I don't know what we would do without you.

Carol and Pat

Reflection of April 6, 2004

Kevin has lost 22 pounds in the three weeks he has been in Houston – the food, what little he eats, seems to go right through him.

I am at home and will probably return to Houston about the 16th or 17th. Pat will return this Sunday/Easter. What a different Easter this will be from last year!

On Thursday Kevin will see his primary and, according to the lab results, next steps will be decided. Likely it will be to be admitted for his second round of chemo later that day.

Fear is playing a bigger role in all of us this time around. Another thought: one aspect of Kevin and Kathleen's on-going battle with Kevin's cancer that impresses me greatly is their honesty about everything that is taking place. They don't shield each other from the truth. Whenever I have tried to ask Kathleen a difficult question without Kevin knowing, she just sets me straight: "Ask Kevin," or "You can say that out loud, Mom."

I guess that it is in order to save myself the pain of asking questions with likely painful or undesirable answers—and therefore seeming to cause Kevin pain—that I have tried to do that on the quiet. But he and Kathleen have a clear channel between themselves and the doctors.

I know that honesty is the best policy but I can see that I am having a hard time dealing with it.

Email of April 15, 2004

Dear Family and Friends,

I thought we would know more at this point but little seems to have been resolved. We expected that when Kevin saw his doctor last Thursday that he would probably be admitted to the hospital to begin his second cycle of chemo. Somehow he was not told that these cycles are 28 days long, not 21. He saw his doctor today, day 28, but it was decided that his "counts" were not high enough for him to be admitted to begin his second cycle. Nor were they appropriate to go ahead with the bone marrow transplant. His next testing will be on Tuesday, the 20th. The problem is that his body must produce some good "counts" on its own power, not only through transfusions.

Kevin was supposed to have a CT scan today but the barium wouldn't stay down so they will try again tomorrow. He will also have another lumbar puncture and chemo session tomorrow. Nausea and vomiting have been real problems for him this time around.

On the side of good news: Kathleen, Connor and KerryAnne have moved bag and baggage to Houston and are all settled. We have also been blessed with some very special people, Chris and Kitty, who live in Houston and have become family to all of us. It is an incredible comfort and grace to have them in our lives.

Kevin's brother Patrick was in Houston this week. I will be going this Saturday and stay for two weeks. As helpful as it is to have someone with them, I think it must also be very difficult to never be alone as a family.

This time in Houston has been much more difficult for Kevin. Nausea and vomiting can ruin anyone's day. On top of everything else his body is experiencing, it is a real cross.

May Kevin's body respond in a healthy way so that his treatment may continue toward that miracle of full health that we fully expect. And, in all things, thank God for his goodness to Kevin and all of us.

With our love and gratitude,

Carol and Pat

Email of May 2, 2004

Dear Family and Friends,

This last week brought some progress and decisions: Kevin will enter the hospital on Tuesday or Wednesday of this week to begin the transplant process; his brother Patrick has been selected as the donor. Kathy and Susan also matched (a phenomenal bit of good luck) but Patrick was chosen because of the gender match.

Patrick will fly to Houston on Monday. On Tuesday he and Kevin will meet with the doctor who will then put Patrick through a rigorous screening to be sure that all is well with *him. Once this is complete, Kevin will be admitted to the hospital. The actual transplant will not occur for a week (about May 11th). During that time Patrick will be prepared for the "harvesting" of his blood stem cells. Kevin will be receiving heavy doses of chemo and be stripped of all immunity so that his body will accept the transplant. He will be extremely vulnerable and will be kept in an isolated area.*

*The **procedure** of the transplant is relatively simple: It is like a blood transfusion and will be administered right in Kevin's hospital room. However, the **process** of the transplant and its grafting, its taking hold, is extended and holds many dangers. Kevin will be in the hospital for a month. Following that he must remain in Houston, within ten minutes of the hospital, for at least two months during which time he will make very frequent trips to the hospital for outpatient care. He will be very vulnerable to infection. Kathleen will be his official caretaker and the rest of us will be supportive over the distance.*

We were all very disappointed, if understanding, when the doctor told them that the children could not stay with them after Kevin is released from the hospital. He will be in such a weakened state that it would not be safe for him. They will return to South Florida where Grandma Grace is going to take over the baby-sitting (I am afraid there is not much "sitting" involved at this stage!) with plenty of assists from all the family down here and Kevin and Kathleen's wonderful neighbors.

I just returned from Houston yesterday. Kevin looked good and his spirits were up. He is as thoughtful and sweet as always. He has lost 30 pounds so nothing fits him and the doctor said he can expect to lose 15% of his present weight during this process. Just think of all the wonderful fattening foods he will be able to eat when he recovers!

The children are so dear! Connor's vocabulary has just exploded! He repeats everything he hears, loves to read, and can sit and play with his "little people" and cars for great periods of time. KerryAnne is rolling over, "talking" a great deal, and is very attracted to bright colors and jewelry (a real girl!). Kathleen and Kevin are considering the possibility of video phones so that they can all see each other over this time apart.

We feel great confidence that Kevin will have a very good outcome. He IS a "miracle in progress." Ask and thank God for this blessing of the fullness of health for Kevin. We know that Kevin, and all of us, are supported by your love and prayers.

Would you also remember Kevin as you sit down to your evening meal? That was always our family's special time together where we felt we built so much of our strength. We now need your strength added to ours.

May God bless and keep each of you in His tender care.

With love and gratitude,

Carol and Pat

WINGLESS ANGELS EVERYWHERE

In times of crisis or tragedy, those at the center of it are often told "Please let me know if there is anything we can do," and those words are sincerely spoken. But it is far more helpful to hear of some small, specific action that the speaker will initiate. A quote I came across recently says this well: "The smallest action is greater than the biggest intention."

When Kevin and Kathleen first arrived in Houston, their immediate needs were met by Kitty and Chris, archangels of the first order whom you have already met. But others also stepped up. After their introduction at the Mass in Rice University student center, DelRena and Jim offered them their condo for the coming three months while they would be away. A visit with them made it obvious that it was just too luxurious to be occupied by a couple with an active toddler. But how could you not be touched by such generosity!

Natalie had known Kevin since his infancy. She now lived in San Antonio with her husband and made a number of trips to Houston, bringing a touch of home and a bit of cheer to hospital visits, as well as household items that would be needed.

Kevin's crisis evoked helpful responses from every corner of the country. In one of those cases, Kevin and Kathleen started receiving cards and notes of encouragement from a small town in North Carolina. We were bewildered until some sleuthing helped us to discover that a distant cousin-in-law belonging to a small church there had mentioned Kevin's plight. That small congregation decided to do what they could beyond prayer and try to lift his spirits by the "card ministry" they initiated on his behalf. A steady stream of mail filled Kathleen and Kevin's mailbox with hope.

There is in all faith communities an encouragement to "give of yourself", and not just by your prayers. At one point, a scheduled blood transfusion for Kevin was cancelled because there was no blood of his type available. When I mentioned this in an email, we were humbled to receive several offers to fly to Houston to donate the blood Kevin needed. Some gifts are indeed awesome.

Not all offers of help fall into that category but all are important and spirit-lifting. Pat and I both had co-workers and colleagues who connected us to doctors or information that might offer some insight or help. Most of these did not pan out, but we were still grateful. Pat's colleague Steve urged us to stay in his home, closer for us by an hour to Good Samaritan Hospital when Kevin returned from Houston the last time. From others came offers of financial aid or of frequent flyer points to help with the many trips between Florida and Texas.

Our friend Denis was a volunteer in a federal prison camp in the Midwest. He had shared Kevin's story with the prisoners he served, and they took Kevin under their wings spiritually rooting for him. He wrote they were "distraught" when Kevin expired. It is one thing to hear of the prayers of churchgoing friends, but quite another to be jarred into an awareness of the common humanity we share with others who are living a life quite different from the one we know, in jails and prisons.

Many well-intentioned, faith-filled friends spoke of Kevin's fight with cancer in terms of "God's will". It is impossible to think of a loving God in such terms and we could never accept that thought. As you might imagine, we were profoundly touched by this message that came at another time from Denis: "God's nature is to heal, and at the darkest moments His loving presence is with Kevin and each of you." His message came at one of those "darkest moments" and we took it in greedily and absorbed its comfort.

Words do make a difference. They especially meant a great deal to me. The emails I sent out often prompted responses full of love, encouragement and support that I desperately needed to hear. They sustained me through many difficult, discouraging days when I teetered on the edge of helplessness and hopelessness.

Even the smallest of gestures offers a boost to your strength and hope when they may be running low.

You may not believe in heavenly sorts of angels but I can assure you that many who have no wings surround us.

PAT'S STEM CELLS

The procedure that we hoped would not be required became a necessity. Kevin would need a stem cell transplant. All of our children had been tested. Kathy, Susan and Patrick had all been found to be compatible, an unlikely bit of luck. Ultimately, Patrick was chosen because of the additional commonality of gender.

The first part of the process was the harvesting of his stem cells. In preparation for that, Patrick spent two weeks in Houston receiving a powerful drug that forced his body to produce a large amount of white blood cells from which the stem cells were extracted.

During those two weeks Patrick, Kevin and Kathleen were in the Houston apartment doing the usual everyday things. There was never any talk of the possibility of Kevin not receiving them successfully. Patrick never gave serious thought to that possibility, or believed it would come to that.

On the day of the actual harvesting of Patrick's stem cells, he sat in a recliner chair with his arms extended, strapped to boards which would prevent any movement. A needle was placed in a vein in each arm. The blood that flowed out entered a centrifuge that separated its components, removing the stem cells and then returning the "leftovers" into Patrick's other arm.

Kevin sat with Patrick throughout the eight-hour process, offering distraction with conversation, and help in whatever way he could offer it.

Patrick's main thought throughout that day and the weeks before and after was: "I felt I was going to save him."

Email of May 16, 2004

Dear Family and Friends,

We have heard from some of you inquiring as to Kevin's progress. I haven't written before because there was another delay. Due to a mix of reasons we do not fully understand, Kevin's admission into the hospital was delayed a week which means that it took place this last Wednesday evening instead of the previous week. But things are now on track again.

Our son Patrick was in Houston for almost two weeks and his blood stem cells were successfully harvested. They have been frozen, the typical procedure at MD Anderson. Kevin will receive the transplant this Wednesday, May 19th. We know that all of you have been praying with intensity during these days. We are sure that those prayers will be put to good effect this week. Kevin has been receiving very heavy chemo in preparation for the coming transplant.

We all feel eagerness to get on with the procedure and all the benefits it can bring but anxiety too at the danger involved. Kevin, most of all.

Please pray for whatever Kevin's greatest needs are, as only his Heavenly Father can know them. And for Kathleen's. And that the Divine Physician may guide and bless with wisdom all the medical personnel involved in caring for Kevin.

We remember each of you in prayer with both gratitude and love.

Carol and Pat

Email of May 19, 2004, from Kathleen

Hi Everyone,

Kevin received his transplant this morning — so now we have to watch and wait to see what happens. So far he seems to be okay; he has had some nausea and a few other minor side effects from the chemo he received but other than that, he seems fine. The whole transplant procedure was pretty uneventful, taking about an hour and a half from start to finish. Now we just have to wait and see how his body reacts.

As I get more information to pass along, I'll send it to you. Thank you all again for your thoughts, prayers, calls and good wishes!!! And please feel free to pass this on to anyone that I might have missed!

Love,

Kathleen

Email of May 24, 2004

Dear Family and Friends,

The hardest part of being a parent who has a child in crisis is coping with the sense of helplessness, of powerlessness, of our inability to affect the outcome ....

Kevin did receive the transplant last Wednesday after a week of massive chemo treatments. He has had several bad days. He is having a very hard time with pain, nausea, vomiting, and a very sore throat. He has received platelet transfusions twice in the last three days and is still on a down swing. In some ways this is to be expected but it seems worse than we anticipated. We know that his body has to be defenseless so that Patrick's blood cells can be accepted and the bone marrow regenerated. We will not begin to know the outcome until the end of this week.

The next ten days will test Kevin in every way. Please pray that he will be relieved of these painful symptoms; that all who care for him will be guided by the highest wisdom, that there will soon be encouraging signs of Kevin's return to health. I feel so inadequate to even know what to ask for but I know that God will read our hearts in asking for all that is good for Kevin.

Email of May 25, 2004

From Kathleen

Hi Mom,

I talked to Chris and Kitty on Sunday morning about being able to help me out next week until Heather gets in and I think it will work out to have their help after school. Given the last minute timing and expense of getting a flight at this point, don't worry about flying out next week; I think that we'll be okay. It's not that long a period of time between Kathy and Heather, and I think that Kevin will start to feel better by then as well. I also don't mind having a few days without company in the apartment, as well as just some time by myself with the kids since this will probably be the last chunk of one-on-one time that I'll get to spend with them for a couple of months ….

I hope to decide by the end of this week when I am going to fly the kids home. I have just been trying to get a good handle on how Kevin is recovering and such as we wait for his counts to start to rebound. Other than that, he is still feeling pretty crappy. He has been very nauseous and has had a pretty sore throat. They took him down to x-ray his lungs today as a precaution to look for any sign of pneumonia. They are also doing blood cultures this afternoon to check for any other sign of infection. He is being transfused with red blood cells today as well. He has been doing some walking and he has been doing his breathing exercises and a few other exercises in bed that he can do without feeling quite as nauseous. He really hasn't eaten much but they're not pushing the issue either since his throat is pretty raw. As long as he keeps taking fluids (which he has been), the doctors will be happy with that until he starts to feel better. They have been keeping him on a pretty constant low dosage of pain medication for his throat, so he has been pretty sleepy/groggy most of the time that I'm here with him.

I'm going to run since the nurse is coming in with more medical goodies for Kevin. Please feel free to forward this on to the rest of the family. I'll talk to you soon!

Kathleen

Email of June 8, 2004

Dear Family and Friends,

I didn't have the heart to write until I had something encouraging to share with all of you. The good news is that after two tortured weeks, things are looking up! Kevin has suffered a great deal, all of it coming under the heading of "side effects" from the chemo. The first harbinger of good news came a couple of days ago when his white blood cells began to inch up. His throat is no longer sore and raw, the rash is 90% gone, the constant nausea has subsided. He ate his first solid food in eight days yesterday! He is very weak and fatigued but so much, much better than he was a week ago.

Kevin has had some tests which indicate that he has the Graft Versus Host Disease (GVHD). It is not unexpected since a great percentage of patients do experience it. It comes in a great variety of intensities, from acute to chronic and we pray that his version will be mild and passing. Almost everything he has experienced until now has been due to the chemo. Now his body will be in a struggle over the transplant itself — whether the transplant (the graft) will "take" or be rejected by the host (Kevin). That is now the challenge.

On Wednesday I will be heading out to Houston to prepare to take over the watch. Kathleen will be returning to West Palm Beach with the children in anticipation of Kevin's release from the hospital. (Once the children are settled in at home with Grandma Grace, Kathleen will return to Houston and I will return to Miami.) He still has a ways to go before he can return to their apartment but we want to be ready. Once he is released he will be required to be within ten minutes of the hospital for the next two months. He will probably be in the hospital on a daily basis as an outpatient for the first few weeks and then gradually reduce those visits as he regains his strength. He has a long road to recovery.

These days, so full of anxiety, fear and helplessness, have been made immeasurably more endurable due to your notes, cards, calls, emails, hugs and prayers. It would truly be Hell to face this alone — as some must. We encourage you to extend your prayer coverage to all who find themselves in serious health situations.

As you remember Kevin in your prayers, think of Kathleen also. She has been a tower of strength for all of us, especially Kevin. We don't know how she has managed so well but we are full of admiration for her steadfastness, her optimism and can-do attitude.

Kevin has more than a few hurdles to cross in the weeks ahead and we count always on your prayers. And we assure you of a grateful remembrance in ours. We are convinced there is a good outcome ahead. God bless you and all those you love!

Email of June 25, 2004

Dear Family and Friends,

It is such a joy to be able to send along to you the good news that the transplant is taking! Yesterday Kevin's doctor told him that a high percentage of Patrick's blood cells have been observed in his blood. That may not be the technical wording but it makes the point! The transplant is taking place. We also learned that the CT scan of his torso taken on Wednesday came back clear and the blast cells (cancer) in his bone marrow remain at 1% (normal is between 0 and 5). It was a good day! For which we thank God. The success of the transplant is the first big step in Kevin's recovery. Staying in remission is the remaining challenge.

The only negative note is that the steroids have caused Kevin to have Diabetes type 2. He must give himself insulin three times a day. This is temporary but he must be careful not to hurt himself since stopping the bleeding would not be easy. His platelets remain on the low side.

The rest of this note is just detail that you may prefer to skip. The big news is at the top!

My time with Kevin in Houston was good. He was released from the hospital just as I arrived and Kathleen left for Florida with the children. He is very thin and fatigues easily but each day I was there his appetite improved, his walks increased in length and his step seemed a bit more confident. Stairs pose a real challenge for the time being since the steroids have had a very deleterious effect on his muscles. Every little improvement is a milestone to be celebrated.

Whenever Kevin leaves the apartment, he wears a surgical mask to protect himself from infection. Any place else it would draw quizzical looks but here in Houston chemo patients are everywhere so it seems as though no one even notices.

For the time being, Kevin is making daily trips into the hospital where he is assigned a room for his four-hour transfusion of liquids and whatever drugs are required according to his daily blood draw. If his red blood cells or platelets are low, it could mean another couple hours for those infusions. The Nurse Practitioner who is attached to his doctor sees him every day, checking on symptoms, adjusting his meds and answering questions. His doctor sees him once a week.

*Thank you for bringing Kevin to this point, for accompanying and supporting all of us who love him, on this journey. The road remaining is still a long one. For myself, I find that I must fight fear at every step, that the joy is never untainted. But **this is a great step in the right direction so let us celebrate!***

✉ *Email of July 5, 2004*

Dear Family and Friends,

Kevin was hospitalized this evening. He has developed an increasingly painful rash. A rash is the most common symptom of Graft Versus Host Disease (GVHD). Over the last few days he has described it as "very painful" — a term he has seldom used. He has the rash on his arms and legs but the most painful areas are his back and neck. The rash is spreading and intensifying at a rate that the doctors feel requires hospitalization. In admitting him they will be able to administer stronger medications intravenously, as well as manage his pain better.

The transplant and Kevin's body are in conflict. We had hoped it would be otherwise.

It is difficult and awkward to send news like this. How many times can we cry "wolf"!? But we are encouraged because we know you care and because you have already invested much prayer in his recovery. Do not feel obligated to reply, but please do pray. We know God has his plan for Kevin and we trust in that plan and in his love. Pray for the brilliant, wise and caring doctors and nurses, for miraculous medicines, for strength and energy for Kevin and Kathleen. We make this prayer in the all-powerful name of Jesus.

Carol and Pat

*** If you prefer not to receive these emails, we would understand and not be offended. Please don't hesitate to let us know if that is the case.

Email of July 14, 2004

Dear Family and Friends,

The rash that was so painful for Kevin was eventually diagnosed as shingles, an infection of a nerve. To clarify *things further, Kevin actually has two rashes, one caused by the shingles, and the other caused by the Graft Versus Host Disease. As painful as the shingles are, it is preferable, by far, that his pain came from that infection rather than the GHVD. GVHD that caused as much pain as Kevin experienced carries many more significant and long lasting implications. It is a very unusual set of circumstances when someone can say, "Thank God, it's only shingles!"*

Kevin had an unexplainable experience when he was at his worst. At that time everything he did took an enormous effort whether it was picking up the phone, eating, or trying to stand and walk. He was nauseous, confused, in great pain, and felt that he was going downhill. He felt prompted to do something to change things and started exercising in bed — leg lifts, arm curls and other simple movements. He was able to continue for about 30 or 40 minutes and said that by the time he stopped he felt totally better and clear headed!

I am sure that there is an explanation for the shift in his condition, somewhere, but I am convinced it was the result of grace, of all the prayer being offered for him. It was one of those moments of crisis, of opportunity and danger — and the positive won out!

Kevin is now at home. He is taking 15 different medications each day and stays close to home when he is not in the hospital for outpatient care.

(During a recent visit, Kevin received the usual three-month supply of a new very, very costly drug which must be refrigerated. He pointed it out to me saying, "There is my BMW." It seemed to us then and now that the practice of sending 90 day supplies is a poor one. All of those drugs were required to be jettisoned when Kevin's transplant failed a month later.)

On Monday night when we spoke with Kevin he told us of another Bone Marrow Transplant patient who was near the end of her 100 days in Houston, has relapsed, and is going back to her home state. That kind of news is very sobering.

*As I wrote to someone recently, this whole process feels like being on an out-of-control roller coaster ride. It is only faith that assures us that no matter what it feels like, things are **not** out of control. Our thanks for all the ways you support Kevin, Kathleen and all of us. No matter how it is you reach out to us, it is a comforting, healing, loving touch that we receive with great gratitude.*

We remember you and your loved ones in our prayers.

Email of August 12, 2004

Dear Family and Friends,

This is so difficult to write. We spoke to Kevin earlier this afternoon. He told us that his doctor had informed him that his blood work indicated that he has relapsed. He will have a bone marrow aspiration later today or tomorrow to confirm those results. His doctor told Kevin that he has two choices: to come home and pass a month or two with his family, or to be taken off the steroids that are fighting the GVHD. That would give him a 10 to 20% chance of success but he would have to stay in Houston.

This information is very incomplete and perhaps I should wait for more before writing but I can't. I will send another email as soon as we do know more.

In the meantime, we ask for your prayers for that miracle we have always believed to be in progress. It takes a bit more faith to still believe in it, but we do believe. Pray with us for it.

Carol and Pat

Email of August 14, 2004

Dear Family and Friends,

This afternoon Pat and I, Kathleen's mother and Connor and KerryAnne will be on a plane headed for Houston. The next few days will be critical as Kevin and Kathleen meet with doctors and decide on options. As yet they do not have any further test results.

In these circumstances, it is often difficult to be in touch with people who are in crisis because we feel anxious about what to say. But I want to encourage you to contact Kevin if you usually speak with him, or write if that is the usual way you stay in contact. Kevin is a people person and thrives on the interactions with the people in his life. You will not find him morbid. Even at this time, he is not angry and maintains a sense of humor.

This relapse was totally unexpected. Kevin seemed to be doing well so it took us all by surprise. I want to say unequivocally that we have not given up hope that either through science or God's direct intervention, Kevin will live to share a long and healthy life with Kathleen and their children. That is where we ask for your prayers to be directed. We all also need courage and strength and wisdom, and ask for your prayers for those needs.

With our love and gratitude,

Carol and Pat

Email of August 19, 2004

Dear Family and Friends,

We are in Houston with Kevin and his family. We have seen both his bone marrow transplant and lymphoma/leukemia *specialists. There are very few options. We are waiting for Friday when we hope that because of the removal of the immune suppressing drugs, Kevin will start to show signs of Graft Versus Host Disease which up until now we have wanted to suppress. Now our hope is that it will flare up but not so badly that it cannot be controlled.*

When Kevin was a boy and we went camping, he loved to be the keeper of the campfire. He would build it, blow on it, coax it along, fanning its flames. We now need your prayers to fan the sparks in him to new life. BREATHE your energy into him. We need his life force to break out into a new freshness.

Hold Kevin in the Light so that God can see and provide whatever he needs. We make this prayer in the all-powerful name of Jesus. Amen.

Please pass this along to everyone who may have been missed. God bless you.

Email of August 23, 2004

To my dearest children,

The transplant doctor has just informed us that the GVHD possibility no longer exists. He encouraged Kevin to return to Florida as soon as possible, there to opt for home care.

Or, to try chemo in the hospital and get a few more weeks but no hope beyond one percent. We will probably try to get Kevin and Kathleen on a flight tomorrow.

Please be prepared for how Kevin looks. His face is moon shaped and he has many black and blue marks. He has lost a lot of weight and is extremely weak. We have not given up. Lisa is still pursuing possible treatments through the U of Nebraska and U of Washington in Seattle. Kevin is going to ask the doctor for steroids to get/keep the white blood count down. It skyrocketed over the weekend.

Kevin is receiving blood right now.

We know that Kevin is in God's hand now, as he has always been. We must continue to hope and to pray.

All my love,

Mom

MOTHER, BROTHER, FRIEND

Susan had celebrated her tenth birthday the night before Kevin was born. She practically considered him her birthday present. From the first days she hovered over him, cooing and cuddling. She was always ready to tend him in whatever ways he needed. As the months passed she assumed the role of Kevin's "other mother". When Kevin was about six months old, she took on the responsibility of occupying him on Saturday mornings so that I could sleep in for a precious extra hour.

They were always close and as the years passed Sue met, fell in love with and married Steve. Ten years later Kevin met, fell in love with and married Kathleen. Both couples eventually bought homes just two blocks apart in the area of West Palm Beach. Steve and Kevin, both engineers, even worked for the same company and shared daily commutes. In the process they became fast friends.

Kevin's illness converted the entire family's energy and focus into doing whatever was needed to return him to health and to support both him and Kathleen in every way they could. But Sue and Steve were especially affected.

When Kevin returned to South Florida after he had relapsed, I started thinking about the impact on Steve especially. One day I said to him: "Steve, I know that Kevin has been like a brother to you, and watching him suffer this way must be very painful."

Steve's immediate, anguished reply was: "He's not just my brother... he's my brother-in-law... my neighbor... my co-worker... my friend!"

Email of August 26, 2004

Dear Friends,

We were unable to return to Florida earlier this week since Kevin was hospitalized on Tuesday because of bilateral pneumonia and high uric acid numbers. The doctor is working to achieve a window in which Kevin will be stable enough to travel home. Pray for that. After he returns to Florida he will enter the hospital there to receive more chemo in order to try to induce remission and then look for more options.

When he was first diagnosed last year he said he was willing to do anything so that he could be here for his family and he has been true to his word. He has experienced every painful procedure and every setback on the books. With great grace. He continues to be willing to do whatever else is asked of him so that he might live.

Kevin struggles to do everything he can for himself. He has received two units of blood each day this week, and platelets twice. He is on oxygen. He has a tremor in his left arm which may be due to neurological cancer.

Kevin has been the essence of courage and love personified. For me, he is truly a Christ figure. Pray.

Carol and Pat

HELL ON EARTH

That is how I described the last months of Kevin's life. It had been a Hell of a year: chemotherapy, radiation, a bone marrow transplant. Then things got worse, much worse.

Thursday, August 12, Day 85. *Hospital rooms are always cold in order to keep infections down. But there was another kind of chill in the air when Dr. X entered Kevin's hospital room looking very solemn. In essence he said, "Two weeks ago, Kevin, your brother's cells showed in almost all your blood cells and now ... they are gone." Dr. X went from looking solemn to distraught. "I am sorry, so sorry. I can't think of anything we could have done differently. If I could, I would recommend trying the procedure again. I left being an oncologist to become a bone* *marrow specialist because our degree of success is so much greater in this field. I am so sorry."*

Three of Kevin' siblings had qualified as donors. His brother Patrick was chosen because the fact that they were both males seemed to further ensure success. Patrick arrived in Houston to begin his preparation two weeks before the scheduled transplant date.

Wednesday, May 19, Day 1. *In a deceptively simple procedure, the bone marrow transplant (BMT) was accomplished. Simple, yes, but the total process was replete with both peril and pain. The week before it began Kevin received massive amounts of chemo to make his body defenseless and thereby vulnerable to infection, all in an effort to ensure the acceptance of his brother's blood cells. He spent most of the two weeks following the infusion in a state of grogginess from pain medication.*

Tuesday, June 8, Day 20. *Kevin was released from the hospital. Once a bone marrow transplant patient has been discharged, he is required to stay within ten minutes of the hospital for the 100 days after the transplant. During that time there are almost daily trips back to be monitored, tested and treated. As BMT patients gather and wait their turn with the doctor they ask each other: "What day is it for you?" "Day 25." "Day 63." "Day 37." Then, "How are you doing?" and the patients compare notes on how they and their families are coping.*

Thursday, June 24, Day 36. *We learned that the transplant was taking and we were elated but it was a rough ride with good days and weeks interspersed with setbacks. The worst of them was an intensely painful rash that covered Kevin's body for far too many days. It was an unending emotional roller coaster.*

Wednesday, August 4, Day 77. *Kevin was doing well and counting the days until he could leave Houston and return to his home in Florida. He felt so optimistic at reaching this far in his recovery that he had recently made reservations for the annual family Thanksgiving reunion that was now only three months off. Things were looking very good.*

Dr. X continued. "I recommend that when you return to Florida that you do not enter a hospital. Spend your last days at home with your family, in peace."

Even as we absorbed the shock of his words, we could not miss the distress he felt at this failure of science, at the sense of loss and failure he so personally felt. It was cold comfort but we were very grateful for his personal caring.

Fifteen months earlier when Kevin had been diagnosed with Stage IV lymphoma, he had said, "I will do everything I can so that I can be here for my family." And he did. He had the intensity of a 30-year-old with his whole life ahead of him, and he wasn't going without a fight. There was his wife Kathleen to think about, and two-year-old Connor and baby KerryAnne. The treatments were hellish.

If they were administered to an enemy combatant they would be considered "cruel and unusual punishment."

When this final bad news came, as a family we began to run down every lead on any possible treatment. I made calls to the few institutions across the country that offered any hope at all in this area of advanced research, and asked to speak to the doctor directing it. I was amazed to have the most renowned doctors return my calls the very same day and to listen attentively as I briefly described Kevin's circumstances. But each call ended with an expression of regret. "I wish I could offer you some hope." My opinion of doctors shot up to an all time high that day. But our hopes shattered on the hard ground of reality.

We began to prepare to return to Florida, a more complicated task than we had anticipated. Kevin had to be fever-free and stable enough to travel, and the airline had to have oxygen in place for him. Three times arrangements were made and cancelled.

On Friday, August 27, on what should have been the triumphant Day 100 of recovery, the transfer was made. Because he was not about to surrender yet, Kevin was admitted to Good Samaritan Hospital. Soon after his return, he told his sister Susan "I didn't come home to die."

HELL ON EARTH CONTINUES

The return to Florida had taken place in the midst of one of the most active hurricane seasons on record. The next two weeks tested us in new ways.

On Thursday, September 2, Hurricane Frances approached. All patients in Good Samaritan were evacuated to St. Mary's Hospital because it was further inland. Kathleen and Kevin's sister Susan, a nurse, spent three days and nights there with him through the storm. Power was lost at St. Mary's for twenty-four hours and the floor was wet because the window in his room leaked. Eventually there was not even any clean linen available. The only furniture in the room was the bed on which Kevin had been transferred. Kathleen and Susan "slept" in the camp chairs they had brought with them.

Monday, September 6: Doctors told us that a strep infection in Kevin's spinal cord had spread to his blood. The antibiotics they had already tried were not having an effect. They would try one "last chance" antibiotic but offered us slim hope of it working.

Wednesday, September 8: Kevin was fever free during the night and there was hope the latest antibiotic was working but he spiked a temp of 101 that afternoon. He and the other patients were returned to Good Sam later that day.

Thursday, September 9: Kevin was fever free that morning and the doctors believed this infection was history!! Is it any wonder that we all felt what can only be described as giddy with relief?!

During this anguished week, the rest of the family had been hunkered down in two locales sixty miles apart. Six homes had to be shuttered in preparation for the storm. In the midst of it, one of our elderly members experienced kidney failure, and we were divided between two hospitals in two different counties. When the storm passed, the homes in West Palm were without power for seven days. With all that was happening, and all that had to be done, every member of our family was operating on pure adrenalin. The stress of the hurricanes coupled with Kevin's deteriorating condition tore us apart and held us together.

Email of September 9, 2004

Dear Friends,

Kevin has made it over a tremendously high hurdle in beating this infection. He still has to fight the battle of the cancer but this little moment is one we are relishing. He has not been out of bed in almost a week. Some days he has been too weak to speak but today was wonderful — he spoke on the phone to almost everyone in the family. We thank God!

Our whole family, it seems, has been leaping over tall buildings all week. We are spread out over sixty-five miles and two hospitals. We have had to shutter and board up our homes once already this week and now face the prospect of another storm of even greater proportions. But no one has had to face any challenge alone.

Good Samaritan is preparing to evacuate again on Saturday if Hurricane Ivan looks likely to come our way.

It is a gross understatement to say that we have experienced the most stressful week of our lives. I feel as though it has really caught up with me in the last day or two but the turn of events today has lifted all our spirits.

Please continue to keep Kevin and all of us in your prayers. For strength and courage, for wisdom and hope, for healers and healing, and always in gratitude for the countless blessings that are ours.

With our love and gratitude,

Pat and Carol

Thursday, September 16: Hurricane Ivan came ashore.

If written as a piece of fiction, the description of the circumstances of these four weeks would cause it to be rejected as unbelievable. This time tested our mettle, our faith, our endurance and our sanity.

In retrospect, I question how we coped. I can only say that in such times all that any of us can do is put one foot in front of the other and do what has to be done at this particular moment. Relief poured over us like cool water time each time a crisis passed. It felt like stumbling onto an oasis in the middle of the desert, grateful that the possibility of life was renewed.

Then there is faith. How do people survive when they are not blessed with faith? I am not even sure what that means. Maybe it's just faith that somehow, in all of this, that there is a God who cares about us and is providing us with the grace and strength to make it through. I only know we needed it.

Always, though, there was the comfort of being surrounded by family and friends. Kevin had five siblings, and their husbands, wives and children all loved him deeply. Through this entire terrifying sixteen-month ordeal, Kevin was never alone either here or in Texas, and his family had every bit of support and help the rest of us could provide. We had each other. In the midst of our sorrow, we were comforted by, and intensely proud of, our family.

Email of September 20, 2004

To our extended family,

We know you all are wondering how Kevin is doing. It is hard to describe. The infection we thought was "history" — still exists. He has been feverish off and on over the last two weeks. As we now understand it, they are trying to keep the infection "controlled."

Kevin has been flat on his back for a while so you know that means that his muscle strength is nil. He has begun to receive physical and occupational therapy. With the help of a Hoyer Lift he can now usually spend an hour a day sitting up in his bedside recliner chair. He was not eating at all but is now usually having cereal in the morning and soup at lunch. He is constantly being hydrated and has received massive doses of antibiotics. He had two very good days late last week but yesterday seemed to take a step backward and was so weak that he hardly spoke.

The one good bit of news is that for the first time, his white blood cell count rose yesterday. We have been waiting for that since it signals that his body itself is beginning to fight back. We need to pray for the regeneration of all of the marvelous functions of the bone marrow. Kevin is such a fighter. Last week he told the doctor he intends to leave the hospital with his eyes wide open.

I don't know where Kevin draws his strength. Actually, I do — it's the thought of Kathleen, Connor and KerryAnne. I don't know how Kathleen does it either.

But my own strength is at an all time low. Up until these last few weeks, I think I have handled things very well. Now I am just dragging, physically and emotionally. That's probably the reason you haven't heard from me.

That's it for now. Keep us all in your prayers. I know you do. Thank you for your calls.

Love, Carol

HELL ON EARTH ENDS

Tuesday, September 21: Kevin slept lightly, speaking little. That evening as I massaged his feet and legs he said, "Mom, I am going to walk out of here and go to the Palm Beach Deli and Mario's Pizza." When Kathleen came in for her usual night shift his Dad and I left to spend the night in a nearby hotel.

Wednesday, September 22, 2004: Dr. G came in and spoke with Kevin and Kathleen that morning. We received a call from Kathleen to come as soon as possible, that there were "important decisions to make."

In reality, there were no further decisions to be made. All options had been exhausted.

We called Kevin's brothers and sisters. Kathleen called her mother to bring their children for a brief visit. Grace walked in carrying ten-month-old

KerryAnne and holding two-year-old Connor by the hand. As they arrived we left the room. Whatever Kevin may have said I do not know. Whatever he may have felt, I could never bear to consider.

During those last few hours Kathleen sat at this side looking at him with a small sweet smile on her face. Kevin's face was turned toward her and I kept hoping that he would open his eyes to see her. She had supported his fight for his life — for their life — with every ounce of her being. At this moment I could see she was allowing him, with incredible grace, to let go of that life.

With Kathleen, his father and me, and his brothers at his bedside, Kevin surrendered his life at 1:25 in the afternoon.

Email of September 22, 2004

Dear Friends,

I am sitting here trying to put into words a grief that should never be spoken: we have lost our beloved son. Kevin fought the bravest fight. We cannot believe that he is really gone. But his example of how to live life lovingly, strongly and joyfully will always be with us.

Please remember Kevin and all of us who love him in your prayers. We are grateful to God for the gift of Kevin. We thank you for all the prayers you offered for him and us. They brought us strength and courage and comfort.

Carol and Pat

Services will be held in the Wellington area on....

POST MORTEM

Friday, September 24. We celebrated Kevin during a moving wake service. We had always cherished him for his kind, thoughtful, joyful and loving ways, but he was our son. We were overwhelmed as his friends and co-workers came forward and we saw how beloved, how cherished, he was far beyond our family circle.

Saturday, September 25. **Hurricane Jeanne** was about to make landfall.

Kevin's body was brought to his parish church for the last time where his life, so lovingly lived, was celebrated.

Then we rushed off to our individual homes to shutter ourselves in, robbed of even this time when we wanted to be together, to remember, to tell the stories, and to mourn.

Email of October 4, 2004

Dear Friends,

Sixteen months ago, when it first became evident that Kevin was dealing with a very serious illness, I did what every mother would do: I prayed. Almost in the same breath of that first prayer, I began to contact our friends to pray with us that this thing we dreaded would not be. Over the months I asked for prayers for many things, above all, for the miracle of a return to health and a long life for Kevin. Over the months, you joined us and together we petitioned God, expecting that this miracle would surely come.

But it was not to be.

Sleepless nights and days filled with both hope and despair gave me ample opportunity to examine my beliefs about life and death, prayer and God. I have distilled them down to these two: God is good and wants only good for us, and that life is imperfect and needs our help.

We are not angry at God that our prayers for Kevin were not answered in the way we hoped. We wish with all our hearts that it were otherwise but we do not fault God. I believe that his desire for Kevin, and for each of us, is wholeness in body, mind and spirit.

I am no longer as sure as I once was about how prayer works or what it is fair to expect prayer to do. What I do know, beyond a shadow of a doubt, is that all of us, especially Kevin and Kathleen, were blessed with the courage and strength needed to meet the challenges of this terrible time. I know that all of us who prayed were drawn closer to each other, and closer to God.

My second belief is about our shared life on this beautiful, weary little world. I do not believe that Kevin's cancer was willed by God. It was just one of the consequences of living in an imperfect world. Someday, because a great many people will have dedicated their lives to it, a cure for cancer will be found. And many of the other ills that we suffer from may also be cured because people care enough to do the tedious work of research, of peace making, of building community, of lending a helping hand, and of applying band aids and kisses to broken bodies and hearts.

Kevin was one of those people who make the world a better place. He enriched the lives of everyone he knew. He smiled. He loved life. He was full of joy. He was always ready to do whatever he could to make the way easier for someone else. He was a thoughtful, sensitive, caring human being. He was grace under pressure, and he loved his family with every fiber of his being.

If you knew him, you know this is true. If you knew him, if you loved or cared for him, we invite you to honor his memory by doing whatever it is in your power to make life better and easier, more loving for the people within your reach, and by taking joy in every day you are given. Kevin would love that!

Many years ago we took our family to see the movie Oh, God with John Denver in the role of Everyman and George Burns filling in as God. The one scene I have carried away from it is seeing Everyman rebuking God over all the illness, war, misery, etc. in this world and in an exasperated tone asking, "Why, if you are so powerful, why don't you do something about all this?!" God answered, "That's why I gave you each other."

Each one of you that is reading this has shared our journey, its joys and its sorrows. We know that there are literally hundreds of you whose faces we have never seen, whose names are barely known to us, as well as friends of longstanding who have shared much of life with us. God couldn't reach down and put his arms around us. Instead he brought you to accompany us, to support and comfort us, to encourage us, to cry with us. And as you shared Kevin's incredible fight to live, we know that you too were blessed.

That's why he gave us each other.

As there are no words to express deep grief, so there are no words to express profound gratitude. We can only pray that all of you will be richly rewarded in this life and in the next by the One who is the source of all goodness.

Email of September 27, 2004

— from Steve to the family:

I sent a note out to the people of Motorola, last Thursday, regarding Kevin. Many people on this distribution list forward it to others, and by the end of the day, over a hundred people at Motorola shared in our loss.

I just want to take a few minutes to add a few comments.

After I sent the email, I realized I had made a mistake with the first line ("one of the world's brightest lights just turned off"). That light did not turn off, but rather, it now shines down on all of us, even brighter from up above, and from within all of us. He truly had, and will always have, a positive influence on so many people.

Secondly, many people have been wearing the yellow wristbands to show support for Kevin. The saying on the wristbands reads "Live Strong." This saying originally was meant for Kevin to live strong, to fight hard, to give him the strength to battle this cancer. But on Wednesday, early afternoon, I believe that the saying transferred from Kevin to each of us. It is now our turn to "live strong', to find the inner strength to get through this great loss. And it is not just an inner strength ... we need to accept the strength from others, from those around us that love us and those who love Kevin.

And finally, what Father Joe said during the funeral service will forever remain with me. He said (something like) "the more love you feel for someone, the deeper the pain you will feel."

And he IS so loved.

Steve

P.S. One of the managers here at Motorola sent this out to the Motorola family that knew Kevin.

In Praise of a Team Mate

The Physical Design Organization last week sadly noted the passing of one of our brightest team members, both personally and professionally, Kevin Farrell.

Kevin's energy, attitude, and seemingly ever present smile, not to mention his engineering abilities and team contributions, were constants in our demanding workplace.

That brightness and energy will truly be missed.

The passing of a friend far too soon places a burden on our hearts. He takes with him a piece of us all. Reflect and smile, remembering what we were able to briefly share.

In response to Steve's email of that day, our son Patrick answered:

Steve,

Thanks for passing along the note from your Motorola colleague. His words helped me to realize that Kevin's impact extended far beyond our immediate family members. The positive force of his personality brightened many, many lives.

Thanks for sharing your own comments, as well. You have been a great friend and brother to Kevin. I know that his passing will affect you deeply as it will anyone. During these last two years, you and Sue have been a backbone of support for Kevin, Kathleen, the kids and Grace. I thank you for all you have done, which is considerable.

Your words of wisdom have provided me with encouragement and hope. Kevin did live-strong (and love-strong) each and every day of his life. If we do the same ourselves, we will be honoring him. I know of no better way. In doing so, we might, if we are lucky, become more like him … a positive force for kindness and caring in a world that is in desperate need of such qualities. I think he would be pleased.

Live Strong,

Patrick

REFLECTION: CHRISTMAS, 2004

*Instead of a Christmas letter to our friends, this is a letter to myself reflecting back on this saddest of years. Kevin's courageous effort to beat cancer, and his defeat, will always be almost the only thing to be remembered of this year. His body, so beat up by all the treatments he endured, was a thing of beauty in death. His face, now thin, his beautiful lips, small nose, his head bare of any hair — looked like a fine piece of marble statuary from classical times. What was not visible was a heart that was filled with **determination** to live, for his family; with **courage** to endure the pain of all the prodding, probing, sticking and every ignominious assault on dignity that has ever been conceived of; with **thoughtfulness, love, good humor and care** for everyone he met along the way.*

I grieve that I was unable to be more supportive and helpful to him as he transitioned from hope to ... reality? That I could not offer any words of comfort! That I could not smile for him. That I could not come to terms with what was happening and, therefore, could not help him at his time of greatest need. That I could not even pray out loud as he was dying!

The services for Kevin — in the midst of the approaching hurricane — were an appropriate tribute to him and all he was. His secretary and other colleagues from Motorola, Brian's moving tribute, filled in a picture of a side of Kevin we did not know but should have imagined if we had ever thought of him as anything but "our Kevin". Having Chris and

Kitty, who had done so much to "be family" for Kevin and Kathleen in Houston; the Korals; my brother and all his family, as well as Kevin and Kathleen's friends from VT, with us, was a sad but beautiful testimony to him.

It is not quite true that Kevin's death is all that we will remember of this year. Pat and I will always look back with incredible pride at how our family pulled together to do every single thing they could possibly think of to support Kevin, to show they loved him, to ensure that he would recover. That he was never alone in all the months in Houston and in Florida that he struggled to live was no small thing.

Not to be forgotten are all the friends, known and unknown, who through the miracle of email walked with us, prayed with us, rejoiced with us and cried with us. They were my support system. They were what I could "do" — and what I needed — when in every other way I felt so powerless.

One thought I could never bear to allow myself to dwell on was to consider what Kevin was feeling at the thought of not being present to Connor and KerryAnne as they grew. He loved them so very much. The thought of leaving them must have caused him excruciating pain. I want so much to create a memory of Kevin for them. I want them to know what a great human being their father was. I want them to know all the things he did that were so special. I want to be for them everything Kevin would have wanted.

This is such a season of sadness for me; it feels like it will never end.

I feel like a hypocrite. I wrote that beautiful letter in October and meant every word of it. Now I feel as though my life is a lie, that I cannot believe as I did then, cannot act as I urged others to act, cannot live as Kevin would want, joyfully. I just feel such profound grief that everything else has almost ceased to exist. I feel so alone. Abandoned. It is a painful time.

Who would ever believe that this reflection is being written two days before Christmas? There is no joy in my heart.

GRIEVING

One of the most insightful observations about grieving came in a letter of sympathy we received from Brian, a young father a few years older than Kevin. "When a whole family suffers a loss, every member of the family grieves so that the ones you would normally lean on are just trying to deal with their own heartache. I cannot imagine where you can find strength in that type of situation."

FAITH

Faith is elusive. We cannot reason ourselves into believing, into faith. Reason can take us toward it but at some point there is that oft-spoken-of "leap" and we find ourselves on the other side.

I never experienced that. I was born into faith, into believing, in my home and in my church. It was part of my package: female, Catholic, American. Believing was as natural as breathing. For years I believed everything that I was taught, as it was taught. There was a lot about sin and hell fire in those days. It took time for me to sort things out and to realize that what was sometimes presented as dogma was actually just the opinion of the person speaking.

My faith in the loving God I had eventually come to know never faltered. All things considered, that seems so unlikely. I believed so much in the power of prayer. My faith should have been destroyed when, after so much prayer, we still lost Kevin. For some inexplicable reason, it was not. Grace is the only way I can explain it.

At Kevin's wake, Pat stood and thanked everyone he could think of for the endless number of ways they had supported all of us. I was anxious to speak but for different reasons: I felt real terror that I may have damaged, maybe destroyed, someone's faith; that after asking so constantly for prayers for Kevin's recovery, and having failed to have our prayer answered in the way we hoped, I feared I may have caused a crisis of faith.

After Pat spoke I stood before them and said: "Don't blame God for Kevin's death. I don't." I used more words than those few but that was the essence of my message. It may have sounded detached, a cold comment from a grieving mother, but it was the best I could do.

The months that followed after Kevin's death were a time of searching. I read and read and read. My faith wanted answers: What is prayer? Why didn't prayer work? What is it supposed to do? We were taught that it was always supposed to work: "Ask and you shall receive." I had believed all that and it had not *worked.*

Answers came, slowly, eventually. Answers to such deeply held beliefs take time to evolve. There are so many pieces to our questions.

At a campground prayer service we attended sometime in the following year, I heard the preacher say that the Bible says "we should 'give thanks IN all things' — it did not say to be grateful FOR all things." I can't begin to express what his words meant to me except to say that I felt such great relief. I could not imagine ever feeling grateful FOR losing Kevin. But in the midst of our misery I could give thanks IN the fact that he had been in our lives at all. His emphasis was clear and logical and comforted me. This awareness was not at the heart of my questions about prayer and faith but it soothed something in me.

Then one day in reading a book by Anne Lamott, I came across this sentence which jumped out at me: *"Gratitude, not understanding, is the secret to joy and equanimity."*

My spirit had been so agitated, so caught up in the *why* of everything that I could find no peace. Why things happen is on so many levels unknowable and searching for understanding was so frustrating. Here, at last, was the one thought that calmed my spirit: in concentrating my thoughts on all the reasons for gratitude surrounding Kevin's life and death I finally came to find peace. I felt such gratitude in *discovering gratitude.* That sentence is odd but I don't know how else to express it.

I centered my thoughts on what a blessing it was to have had Kevin in our lives for 31 years ... for the countless memories he had created ... for the example he offered ... that I was his mother... that he had brought a special joy to our lives ... and that we had done everything we could think of to preserve his life. I would never understand why Kevin was snatched from life, but I would always be grateful for the blessing he was.

None of it could bring Kevin back to us or ease the pain of his absence. But it did bring me peace.

But the essential questions about faith still eluded me: Why had our prayers not worked?

UN-KNOWING-NESS

Kevin had already suffered through fifteen months of treatment for lymphoma when we brought him back to West Palm Beach "to die," his doctors said. They had done everything they could. But Kev was still fighting — for his life, for his family.

He would allow no suggestion that he was not going to make it. Several weeks earlier he had cut me off when I began to tell him how proud I was of him, how Christ-like I saw him, full of love and compassion and hope. "I'm not dead yet!" he had responded with a spark of anger.

But two or three weeks later, back in West Palm Beach, he had been displaced from one hospital to another because of a hurricane. There he contracted an infection that appeared likely to be fatal — but he beat it back.

"Since this infection, for the first time, I'm afraid."

That was the first and only time I heard Kevin speak of fear. It took me by surprise and I fumbled for a response. I hesitated. "We are all afraid ... none of us knows ... what will happen ... what is on the other side. We just have to trust that we are in the hands of the good God who created us."

What I had wanted was to counter his fears with a firm assurance that there was nothing to fear. But I could only share my own unknowingness. I left him that day feeling that I had failed him.

Not many days later, we sat at Kevin's bedside as he slipped away from us, from this life he loved. And somewhere in that last hour I began to sing the much loved children's hymn: "He has the whole world in his hands, He has the whole world in His hands ... He has Kevin and Kathleen in His hands, He has Connor and KerryAnne in His hands, He has the whole world in His hands."

As I look back on it, I see it as the truest expression of what I believe.

IN THE ABSENCE

The ancient hymn challenges
"Oh, Death, where is thy sting?!"
As if the promise of resurrection
removed the pain of loss!

But I will tell you wherein Death's sting lies:

In the absence
Of memories, not made
Of words, unspoken
Of promise, unfulfilled
Of babes, unborn
Of dreams, unrealized
Of touches, untendered
Of comfort, ungiven
Of wisdom, unshared
Of Joy … quenched.

In the absence of these,
Oh, Death, is thy sting!

June 8, 2005

Reflection of July 22, 2005

We gathered together tonight to celebrate the feast of Mary Magdalene, "we" who usually come together to discuss books. This would be a different sort of night.

Carrie brought forward the items we would need for our ritual: a life-sized, carved wooden head of an African woman, an oversized stainless steel bowl and an extraordinarily large container of honey.

In the spirit of The Secret Life of Bees *we were invited to each pour out some of the honey and rub it into the wooden face and respond to the question, "For whom do you weep?" as Christ had queried Mary Magdalene in the garden on that first Easter morning.*

Eventually it came to me and Muriel turned to me and asked, "Carol, for whom do you weep?" I answered: "I weep for Kevin — and for all the young men and women who die too young in Iraq, and for their parents. And I weep for all the good they could have done had they lived."

As I spoke I rubbed the honey lovingly over every part of that beautiful face. I felt as though I was anointing Kevin's body and regretted that I had not thought to wash his body or honor it with a fragrant oil in the time after his death. It was an unexpectedly powerful moment. A gift.

Email of September 2005:

REMEMBERING KEVIN

Dear Friends and Family,

We are approaching the first anniversary of Kevin's death. As we do so, I find myself reliving last year at this time. Part of that memory is the love, support, friendship and presence of all of you during the darkest days most of us have ever experienced. Our communication was so intense, and your responses so important to me, to all of us. In the days and weeks that followed, I missed the dialogue very much but didn't have the energy or heart to continue. But, then too, its purpose had come to an end.

A year has passed and I thought it seemed important to offer a follow-up: As with all things, both positive and negative, they recede in intensity over time. We are marked by them ... changed forever ... but endure ... one day at a time.

I cannot say that my faith never wavered. Everything I have ever believed was challenged at least temporarily. Essentially, my faith is intact and has been my rock, but it is altered. For one thing, I find it difficult to offer prayers of petition with confidence. On the other hand, I find my main prayer is now one of gratitude for the incredible blessings that have always been ours, and continue. Perhaps that is growth.

As we see friends, the first question always asked is, how is Kathleen? It is good to be able to respond that she is doing well. She has taken a new position and is pleased with how the transition has worked. The children are in a neighborhood daycare and happy. When Kevin first became ill he said that he knew two things about Kathleen before they married: that if he ever became ill, she would take good care of him; and, that she would be a great mother. She has proven him right.

When early on in Kevin's illness it had become clear that he likely had a very serious condition, he had said, "I will do everything I can so that I can be here for my family." He loved his family deeply, passionately. He welcomed any treatment that might help him return to health. He endured many, many, painful procedures, but I never heard him utter a word of complaint. He was determined to live. Somewhere along the way I started to think, to realize, how Christ-like he was. On reflection I thought it was almost blasphemous, or just a mother's love idealizing her son. As time has passed, I have come to believe that my original assessment was true. After all, isn't it the goal of a Christian's life to live and love as Christ lived and loved?

Remember Kevin. When we are with you, do not hesitate to speak of him to us. It will gladden our hearts to know that his memory lingers within you too.

May God abundantly bless you and yours.

With our love and gratitude —

A LIFE OF KINDNESS

How do you ever summarize a life and capture its essence? It is a truism that everyone is thought of as a saint once they have died. While I hesitate to characterize Kevin that way, he was good and kind and thoughtful. Kevin was deeply loved in our family. Being the youngest after a break of eight years, it is easy to understand that this baby was going to be lavished with love. From the very beginning he returned that love. If either Pat or I had him in our arms and the other came close, he would reach over and pull us together in his toddler arms. He had a gift for making people feel loved all of his life.

Soon after he graduated from Virginia Tech and settled down into adult life he came across an article about a teacher whose eighth-grade class had struggled with pre-algebra all week. It was Friday and, on a whim, she announced a break and asked them to take out a piece of paper, write down the names of all the other students in the class, and then write down the nicest thing they could think of about each of them. Over the weekend she compiled the lists, transcribed the comments and added hers.

As you might imagine, the faces of her students lit up when they read the comments, one saying "I never knew I meant anything to anyone." One of those former students died in a wartime action a few years later. In his wallet was found that worn, folded list of that life-changing assignment. At his funeral, other students told of keeping their lists.

Kevin was very touched by the story, and that Christmas he asked each of us to create a list identifying the most beloved quality of every other family member. He assembled the responses and gifted us with them on Christmas Day. I still have mine in my dresser drawer.

About that same time, our daughter Kathy was going through a difficult time. She was also approaching that milestone fortieth birthday. Kevin suggested we create a home video of Kathy's life, important places and people, with each of us sharing favorite memories of her in the video, telling her what she meant to us. He took the initiative in the project, came to each of us once we were camera ready. It was the perfect gift — and became a tradition as each of our children reached forty.

During the years Kevin was an income-producing, tax-paying citizen he also became a blood donor. He had the blood type of the universal donor and he gave frequently — until the time he came to need what he had given.

Tim and Marie remember the many times Kevin drove from West Palm Beach to Pembroke Pines and insisted they take some time away from their young family while he cared for his niece and nephew.

In Kevin's last weeks in the hospital, we could not help but notice that he made every request with a "please", received every treatment or bit of help with a "thank-you", including the woman who usually cleaned his room. It was probably how Kevin always interacted with people, but knowing how weak and in pain he was emphasized for all of us his basic orientation to affirm others.

At Kevin's wake we heard co-workers tell stories of Kevin's many thoughtful actions. We had never thought much about this life so apart from ours, as a professional. He was just Kevin, our son. We should not have been so unaware and so surprised to hear so many heartfelt memories. But we were.

There were so many touching anecdotes. Our Susan expressed our common emotional response when she tearfully commented, "Think of all the memories we won't make because Kevin isn't here!" No observation of what we had lost has ever so captured the anguish I felt.

Life is a series of moments, of our responses to opportunities, to disappointments and challenges, to the joys and sorrows that add up to be the story of who we are. Soon after Kevin's death, Tim and Marie memorialized him at their church on a plaque describing Kevin's as "A Life of Kindness."

Kevin's best friend Brian shared these memories:

The day we moved into Vawter Hall – I can remember the busy-ness around me with all the other students moving into their dorm rooms. Most kept to themselves and went about the business of setting up their lofts, unboxing their computers and unpacking their suitcases...but I remember Kevin introducing himself, noticed his outgoing and friendly personality. There was something about the way he engaged with me and others that immediately put you at ease. You couldn't help but feel comfortable talking with Kevin. He was completely unassuming. I knew immediately that I had found a friend.

A couple of the running jokes: The Miami boy didn't own a winter coat (at least for the first year)! It could be twenty degrees with a foot of snow on the ground and he would be wearing a windbreaker ... He liked to eat his meals in sections: Can't start eating those green beans until he's finished with the mashed potatoes. I teased him often about this.

I was fortunate to have had the opportunity to visit Kevin a few times after he was diagnosed with cancer, both in Houston and in West Palm Beach during his last course of treatment. For me it was deeply moving to watch Kevin handle it all with such maturity and grace. He was always the optimist, and when faced with his own mortality his faith was stronger than ever. To witness his life ... the way he loved his Lord, how he loved others, and how he lived every day with joy in his heart was such a blessing to me and everyone he met.

When I go back and reflect on the poem he read to Olivia and me in his toast on our wedding night, I know that those words came from his heart. He lived those words every day.

"'Accept life daily, not as a cup to be drained but as a chalice to be overfilled with whatsoever things are honest and pure.... Making a living is best undertaken as part of a more important business of make a Life. Every now and again take a good look at something that is not made with hands ... a mountain, a star, the turn of a river. There will come to you wisdom and patience and solace and, above all, the assurance you are not alone in this world.'

"Now I would like to propose a toast and a blessing: To Brian and Olivia, may they grow wise from their experience, and always know their friends and family love them. May their chalice of happiness and joy always overflow, and realize although they earn a living with their hands and minds, that they can live life fully and love unconditionally with the love of their hearts."

I think of Kevin often, and will continue to look back on his life as an example for how I want to live mine.

Anders' memories of Kevin:

Dear Grandma,

I might be accused of being a little biased when I write about Kevin. However, I would remind you that it is not necessarily the case that family members get along, let alone like each other.

I'll just get it out of the way: I adored my Uncle Kevin. He was eight years old when I was born and although he was technically my uncle, he was more of a big brother to me.

Every memory I have of him is a good one. How many people can any of us genuinely say that about?

When I was younger we played football, Frisbee and jumped on the trampoline. We played board games and he hosted sleepovers. When I was older we went out to eat and took trips together. There was no shortage of time invested in my life.

Sounds like a good guy, right? Well, he was but it was more than that: he was a living testimony of what I now know is a spirit-filled Christian. Now I assume there were times where anger or some other emotion got the best of him but I'll never know because I didn't see it. He had control of his tongue and his flesh.

When I was 19 or 20 he gave me a Bible with an inscription. He said I may not be ready then to receive the message of the gospel but that he loved me and GOD did too.

Well, he was right. There came a time where I read that bible and cried out to GOD and he heard me. There were other people who sowed seeds in my life but to this day Kevin is the best example of someone I know who "walked the walk".

Every now and then I open the cover of the Bible and re-read the inscription and remember the love of a brother in Christ, my Uncle Kevin.

"For out of the abundance of the heart the mouth speaks" Matt 12:34. "But the fruit of the Spirit is love, joy, peace, forbearance, kindness, goodness, faithfulness, gentleness and self-control."

Love, Anders

Charles' memories of Kevin:

Uncle Kevin was a significant role model for me even though I never consciously thought of him that way. I remember celebrating his graduation from Virginia Tech. He graduated as an engineer and so when my parents said I could be an engineer too I thought it was a great idea.

While growing up, Uncle Kevin helped bridge the gap between my generation and my parent's generation. If the family went out to a restaurant, usually after Saturday bike rides, it was Uncle Kevin that took the time to play with us kids outside before and after we finished eating so the grown-ups could talk. It seems like a little thing now but this probably happened for years and it was fun to have his company and supervision. It was Uncle Kevin that gave me his old road bike so I could ride with the men on those Saturday mornings. Crazy enough, that bike is still sitting in my parent's garage and I think of him when I see it.

One other vivid memory I have is when he arranged a camping trip with Anders, Uncle Tim and me. It must have been during the summer because I don't remember worrying about school. We went to Highlands Hammock, our favorite state park for a couple nights. There was one tent for the four of us and we had all the normal camping gear like sleeping bags and pads, food, water, flashlights, etc. I don't remember all the details but I do remember that it rained most of the days we were there. We put up tarps to help with cooking and I remember having to eat in the car.

Being the smallest of the four guys, I had the honor of sleeping at the lowest part of the tent those nights. I remember waking up very early in a small puddle of rain water that had accumulated. None of the other guys were wet and they found my situation very amusing, of course! In spite of everything this was a wonderful chance to be with my uncles and cousin.

I will always remember Uncle Kevin as a fun and loving man.

MY FAITH JOURNEY

"The older I get, the less I am sure of," he said. "He" was Father Seamus, long-time friend who had shared much of our adult life and been especially present during the last painful month of our son Kevin's battle with cancer. In the time that followed he listened to my questions and my doubts. Where to some, his words might have shaken their faith, they affirmed mine, and comforted me.

My formal education was totally in Catholic schools. I grew into adulthood seeing the world and its problems in crisp black and white. No gray edges. But things began to blur once we moved from the Midwest and encountered the world beyond my Catholic enclave. Living in Miami, a young married mother of four children, I sought out a Great Books discussion group and found one. It was composed entirely of retired Jewish professionals who adopted me with open arms. Over the eight years I met with them, their insights and questions forced me to examine all my beliefs. I became, for the first time, an adult Catholic. I am beyond grateful for the maturing experience these dear friends provided.

I believed in a God who created us in love and wanted/wants what is good for us. I still do. When bad things began to happen to good people whom I loved, it was natural for me to resort to prayer. After all, doesn't Scripture say, "Ask and you shall receive, knock and it shall be opened to you"? As a child, we had a prayer for everything: that it would not rain on our picnic, that the boy we thought so cute would notice us, that we would receive the longed-for gift from Santa, that a relative who had "fallen away" from the Church would return to the sacraments, that we would meet and marry the man of our dreams. Nothing was beyond prayer.

It was the most natural thing in the world then for me to "storm heaven" with my prayers when Kevin was diagnosed with lymphoma. I didn't stop with just *my* praying for his cure; I enlisted the prayers of everyone I knew and everyone they knew. Almost every conversation I entered into, even with strangers, inevitably ended with me telling them about Kevin's plight and asking for their prayers. I was sure we would bring about the miracle of Kevin's return to the vibrant life he had once lived.

But I was mistaken. After sixteen months of every conceivable, torturous treatment the best medical facility in the world could offer, Kevin died.

The human mind is a strange thing. I had watched Kevin diminish day by day during his last days until he could not even move his leg. But he was so determined to live, even up to the night before he died when he said, "Mom, I am going to walk out of here and go to the Palm Beach Deli and Mario's

Pizza." I still believed that we would get the miracle we were praying for, even when all the physical evidence before us clearly showed the contrary. Less than a coherent thought, it was an expectation.

The months after Kevin's death sent me into a frenzy of reading. I wanted to know "why." *Why* had this happened to someone so young, so good, who had so much to live for? And *how* could his body so betray him when he didn't drink, didn't smoke, never took drugs, and was an extraordinary athlete?

It still amazes me that I never doubted God's existence, or His love. But I did question mightily what I had been taught about prayer. When I thought about it, I realized that the teachings I had absorbed reduced God to a vending machine: prayer in, miracle out.

Two books helped me to clarify my thinking and recover a measure of sanity. In *When Bad Things Happen to Good People,* Rabbi Kushner wrote that there is a randomness to life: things happen, none of which are necessarily ordained by God or part of a Divine plan. It is just Nature at work.

Some of the most painful moments during Kevin's illness came from well-meaning, faith-filled people who intended to comfort us by saying, "This is God's will." We wanted to reach out and throttle them and scream, "What kind of God wills this kind of suffering!"

Kushner also questioned what kind of God it would be who would provide a miracle on behalf of Kevin because a thousand people prayed for him, but ignore Joe because only three prayed for him?

What kind of divine justice would that be? It made sense to me.

He wrote that what we can expect from God, and of our prayers, is the strength and courage to deal with the challenges we face.

I do not doubt that miracles can happen and, in rare instances, do. But we don't have the right to expect them—no matter how hard we pray. What came back to me was old wisdom: Prayer doesn't change *things*; it changes *us*.

Rabbi Kushner put it this way: "In your desperation, you opened your heart in prayer, and what happened? You didn't get a miracle to avert a tragedy. But you discovered people around you, and God beside you, and strength within you to help you survive the tragedy. I offer that as an example of a prayer being answered." To which I respond, "Amen. Amen. It is so. It is so."

The Book of Job provided a different insight. For almost forty chapters, Job rails at God over and over again that he was a good and just man and didn't deserve his fate. In the last three chapters, God answers him thunderously beginning with:

"Who is this that obscures divine plans with words of ignorance? Gird up your loins now, like a man; I will question you, and you tell me the answers! Where were you when I founded the earth? Tell me, if you have understanding. Who determined its size, do you know? ... And who shut within doors the sea, when it burst forth from the womb ... and said: 'Thus far shall you come but not farther, and here shall your proud waves be stilled!'" (Job: 38, 2-11)

In essence, God's response to Job comes down to this: "As the heavens are higher than the Earth, so are my ways higher than your ways and my thoughts than your thoughts." (Isaiah 55:9)

In the end, the believing person must yield to the truth of that: I am, and I do.

Instead of full circle, I have come 180 degrees. Who am I to think that I can understand Divinity? Certitude is the prerogative of the young. Where I was once sure of everything, I am now certain of little except this: that we are, in Mitch Albom's words, "frail parts of something powerful."

And that is enough for me.

WHY WRITE? WHY NOW?

Since the time we lost Kevin, I have wanted to write his story. It is difficult if not impossible to explain a delay of fourteen years. Grief is part of the answer. Recalling painful memories has a price. Procrastination is likely another part. As we marked the most recent anniversary of his death, I felt an urgency, a compulsion to begin organizing the materials and commit to the task. I was surely motivated by the very real question which haunts many of my days now: "How much time do you think you have?"

Above all, I wanted to preserve our memories for Connor and KerryAnne, who could only have the stories and experiences that those who had shared life with him could convey. My other goal was that a reading of Kevin's response to his day-to-day challenges would reveal to them the essence of the father they had been deprived of knowing, and the depths of his love for them.

I am breathless at how the years have flown by. Kathleen has poured herself into these two who were brought into life by the love she and Kevin shared. Her determination, wisdom and energy have yielded two young people of which she, and we, can be very proud. And we are.

* * *

As the writing of Kevin's story came nearer to the end, another loss and tragedy was unfolding within our family. Our daughter Kathy's husband Syd was fighting, and then lost, his three-year battle with colon cancer. Almost anyone else would have succumbed in half the time, but Syd was a fighter. He loved and savored life even on the days that were terrifyingly painful. And there were plenty of them.

Syd was intelligent, informed, opinionated, loud and blessed with a memory that held tightly to everything he had ever learned. He was the go-to person before there was Google. It could be absolutely maddening to disagree with him, because his breadth of knowledge was so wide, and his voice so loud and authoritative. You could count on the fact that any "discussion" with him would be extended and volatile.

He had the same energy and enthusiasm for living, for the gift of life, that he had for learning and debate. He knew how to squeeze the juice out of every day. Many is the party that I hosted, worrying every detail, caught up in the doing of it that I hardly enjoyed it, that Syd would interrupt my scurrying about to remind me to relax and enjoy this gathering of people we both loved. I was a slow learner, but he was a persistent teacher.

He had what only be described as a joy in living that was best expressed in his favorite quotation from Marcus Aurelius: "When you arise in the morning, think of what a precious privilege it is to be alive—to breathe, to think, to enjoy, to love."

Syd and Kevin shared that quality of joy but expressed it in different ways. Kevin's way was low key, under-the-radar kindness and compassion. For Syd it was "out there" for all the world to see.

How blessed we have been to have had two such special people in our lives.

LIFE AFTER KEVIN

For a while it felt as though beauty and joy did not exist. We each felt raw, and it showed.

The first year was very difficult. We remembered what was happening on each date of the previous year. As we lived each day we mourned his absence. "Kevin should be here with us." Thanksgiving was especially painful. We gathered as usual for the weekend of camping, but we were a somber group.

Lifetime friends visited with us about six months after his death. I remember fixing dinner with Mary Ann and feeling and acting irritated over the amount of pasta she had suggested we prepare. She and I were very close and had never disagreed over anything. This was so totally unimportant! I could only look back and recognize months later how emotionally shattered and fragile I was. Lucky for me, Mary Ann understood. There are undoubtedly other examples that family and friends could recount.

Life goes on. Pain dulls. Memories persist. Good memories continue to be made, especially at all the different tables we gather around to share the latest mile marker: a birthday, a graduation, a wedding, a confirmation. He is always present because of his absence. We don't wallow in our missing him, but we are ever mindful of him. Thinking of him in these gatherings reminds us to enjoy these precious times we have with each other. We want to remember and honor his memory with joy.

For whatever we have gained—in strength, in love, insight or perspective — none of it can compare with the loss of all that Kevin was for us.

I often recall Kevin's eight-year-old wisdom about speaking our love for each other because "love will make them stronger." We are all stronger as individuals and as a family because of Kevin, because of who he was, how he lived, how he suffered, how he loved so deliberately and generously.

He left us an incredible legacy.

POSTSCRIPT FROM 1983

It was the Friday before Easter 2020. In the aftermath of a move into our new home, we had been busy over the last weeks going through boxes and boxes of the memorabilia of a lifetime: birthday cards, handwritten letters from long ago, children's drawings and report cards. Each one lingered in our hands for at least a long moment before we pitched it into the recycle pile. Perhaps 20 percent made the cut and were tucked away to be revisited.

The bin of recycled material is hauled away every Friday morning. Occasionally, stray pieces float away as they are caught by a breeze as they are lifted into the truck.

On that Friday afternoon, Pat noticed a colorful, frayed piece of paper in the middle of the walk leading up to our door — perhaps thirty feet from the street. As he turned it over in his hands he saw that it was a child's bit of artwork: an Easter greeting — drawn for us — by Kevin. "I love you." In a small penciled notation in the bottom corner was my handwriting: Easter 1983.

The incredible coincidence of finding this greeting on Easter weekend, and having it blown up towards our home seemed incomprehensible. Even more unlikely was the fact that neither of us had ever seen this before — and would never have thrown it away! But here it was in our hands. It seemed to all of us a small miracle — as though Kevin was reaching down and touching us with his love — over time, over space, over eternity, letting us know that no matter where we go, he is still with us.

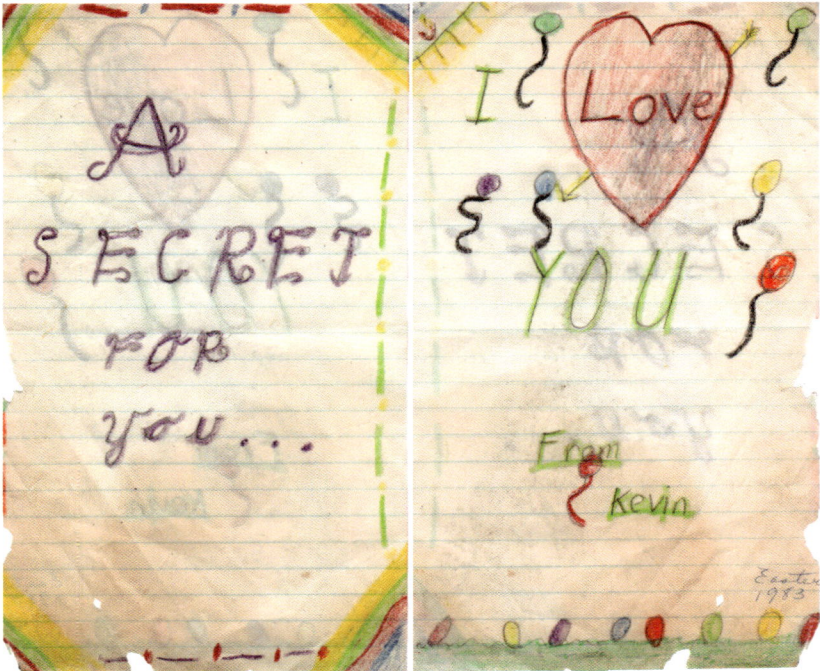